YALE INSTITUTE OF SACRED MUSIC

Colloquium: Music, Worship, Arts

COLLOQUIUM: MUSIC, WORSHIP, ARTS

Published annually by Yale Institute of Sacred Music
Martin D. Jean, *director*
409 Prospect Street
New Haven, CT 06511
www.yale.edu/ism
ISSN 1938-419X

JOURNAL

Editors	Margot E. Fassler and Bryan Spinks
Publication Manager	Melissa Maier
Copy Editor	John Leinenweber
Editorial Assistants	Will Cowen and Robert Bolyard

DVD

Faculty Consultant	Margot E. Fassler
Producer	Jacqueline Richard
Technical Supervisor	Sachin Ramabhadran
Photography/Editing	Scott Libson and Jacqueline Richard

GRAPHIC DESIGN AND PRODUCTION

Maura Gianakos
Yale *RIS*

COVER: Mass at the church in Quoyllur Riti, Mount Ausungate, Peru. Martin Gray / National Geographic / Getty Images. Used with permission.
INSIDE: Detail from a Gotland church. Henri de Feraudy.

Director's Welcome

The world is a shrinking place. The internet, global media, world commerce, and travel have all made information and other kinds of human contact so much easier on the one hand, and so much riskier on the other. The ease is apparent to anyone who has ever opened web browser. The risk might seem more indistinct, except when we think about the errors of assumption we make of one another, both locally and abroad.

For example, in a poll ABC News conducted in 2003, respondents ranked themselves on two scales: their familiarity with Islam, and their perception of whether or not Islam is a peaceful religion. The poll showed that only one-third of Americans felt they had a "good basic understanding" of Islam; of those who said they understood it, 59 percent called it peaceful. In contrast, of the two thirds of Americans who said they were "basically unfamiliar" with Islam, only 40 percent called it peaceful. Even fewer of those people thought that Islam teaches respect for others' beliefs.

This is but one set of misunderstandings that are all too common in our society. Our hope in the Institute is that our teaching, creative work, and research can help remedy this situation in some small way. An examination of ways that cultures define themselves or transform themselves in new contexts is but one approach that you will encounter in this issue of *Colloquium*. We have been inspired and encouraged to assemble this group of thinkers by an already abundant set of initiatives at Yale to think globally, from Yale Divinity School's historic and longstanding commitment to the study of the Christian missionary movement, to the MacMillan Center for International and Area Studies, and the World Fellows Program (our near neighbors located in the Betts House next door), all in keeping with President Levin's overarching vision of Yale as a global university.

The world may be shrinking, but knowledge is expanding exponentially. Understanding needs to expand, too—and so we reach out to understand religions and cultures that are not our own.

We hope that you will find insight and information within these pages that will enlighten your own interpretations of our world.

Martin D. Jean
Director, Yale Institute of Sacred Music
Professor of Organ

Colloquium: Music, Worship, Arts

"The World in Pieces" — so Clifford Geertz entitled his lecture in 1995 to the Institut für die Wissenschaften vom Menschen in Vienna. We used to be able to study culture and inculturation with some sense that we knew what we were talking about, especially when it came to the spread of Christianity throughout the world: Christianity was embodied in the cultures of Western Europe, and carried easily spotted valises with it wherever it went, trunks that were unpacked in various stages, their contents reused, reappropriated, and often thrown out. Now, as the essays in this volume demonstrate in a variety of ways, we know too much simply to look at how a faith tradition must and will be transformed as it moves from one set of "cultural norms" (who could even think in such terms anymore?) to another. To paraphrase Geertz in his lecture cited above, the pervasive raggedness of the world, the shattering of larger coherences, has made relating local realities with overarching ones extremely difficult. "In a spintered world, we must address the splinters."

There could be no better introduction to this volume of essays presented first as lectures to the ISM community in 2004-05, than that provided by the ethnomusicologist Jeffers Engelhardt. He, like Geertz and other anthropologists today, studies what once would have been termed splinters, and so too do musicologists, literary critics, theologians, liturgiologists, art historians, and historians in general. At present there is a rampant need for many to try to define, explain, hold onto the religious values they were inculturated with as children, and people who aren't academics often ask those of us who are why we are saying more and more about less and less, or reifying people and places so foreign to them: "What about us?" But who *are* you?

The Christianity that was sent by missionaries throughout the world is now returning to the West, bags repacked with music, languages, prayers, and expectations, and in the company of other faith traditions as well.

In a world splintered by trauma, and complexified by massive demographic shifts, Engelhardt suggests that we speak about and study processes of change on the edges between peoples who are in fundamental disagreement about their beliefs. This could be a medievalist watching the NASCAR opening ceremonies on a treadmill in the gym, or a Mexican family on its way to their first church service in New Haven. What do these have in common when the people are so different? Some things, perhaps, are human: expectations, different though they may be; reactions to alternity, across a spectrum; the nature of fear of an alien culture appropriating what one knows or of familiar rituals being turned inside out — it is these kinds of things that we look to now, and our authors offer many ways in which to do this, and many ideas about what is learned when we do. As we in the West sing world hymnody while being challenged to the scalps of our own comfort zones by stripes of Christian beliefs we do not recognize, we will change, like it or not; and even if we retreat, it will not be to our familiar hobbit holes in the Shire.

This new issue is packed with many ideas about religion, ritual, music, culture, and change. Take it with you wherever you may travel and become a student of these processes yourself as you go.

Margot E. Fassler
Robert Tangeman Professor of Music History and Liturgy

CONTENTS

YALE INSTITUTE OF SACRED MUSIC

Colloquium: Music, Worship, Arts

VOLUME 3

Inculturation: Genealogies, Meanings, and Musical Dynamics

JEFFERS ENGELHARDT

The richly textured perspectives on inculturation offered in this volume of *Colloquium: Music, Worship, Arts* ask us to revisit and reconsider what is meant by inculturation as an idea, practice, and process.[1] Reading the accounts of Lawrence A. Hoffman, Michael Daniel Findikyan, Philip Tovey, Harold Miller, Bonnie Wade, and Pete Ward of the religious, social, and musical dynamics of inculturation in Armenia and its diaspora, England, Ireland, Japan, and Uganda, as part of global consumer cultures, and in spaces where embodied practices are changing in the face of disease or disability, one quickly appreciates the descriptive and critical value of thinking in terms of inculturation. Inculturation addresses important questions concerning agency, change, translation, consciousness, experience, and efficacy. At the same time, it raises questions about the exercise of power, the relationship of outward expression and inward belief, the nature of religious ideologies and the invariance of religious truths, and how the concept of culture is naturalized and deployed by those engaged in inculturation.

So how have we come to think, hear, and write in terms of inculturation? And what are the possibilities and limits of thinking, hearing, and writing in terms of inculturation? Here I work through these questions by outlining some of the genealogies, meanings, and musical dynamics of inculturation from my vantage point as an ethnomusicologist.

Genealogies

In its conventional sense, inculturation is a thoroughly Christian project, although it can apply to any number of non-Christian contexts when conceived of more generally.[2] Simply put, inculturation is the adaptation or transformation of Christian liturgical expressions and the gospel message under new or changing cultural conditions. In the Catholic Church, for instance, it is the claim, according to Fennela Cannell, "that local forms of approaching God may all be acceptable, and even necessary, as long as the presence of a transcendent deity presiding over all is acknowledged."[3] This often happens within the context of missionization, evangelization, conversion, renewal, migration, and displacement. Therefore, inculturation is intimately related to histories of globalization and encounter,[4] the dynamics of colonial domination and missionization,[5] the asymmetrical relationship between global North and South,[6] and the meteoric growth of Pentecostal and Catholic Christianities outside the West.[7] As the essays in this volume make clear, liturgical and musical practices register processes of inculturation wherever and whenever they occur, and those practices animate the transformative experience of inculturation across many differences.

Modern ideas of inculturation have been shaped by the universal scope of Christian religious ideology, the gospel imperatives of witnessing and evangelizing, the global communication of Christianity through Western ecclesial, social, liturgical, and musical forms, the creativity of new or changing Christian communities, and contemporary discourses of multiculturalism, indigeneity, and rights. Modern practices and processes of inculturation have been shaped by historical moments of translation, adaptation, and exchange between charismatic individuals and non- or newly Christian populations — Saints Cyril and Methodius and their counterparts in ninth-century Great Moravia, Saints Herman and Innocent and their Aleut and Tlingit counterparts in nineteenth-century Alaska, and Roberto de Nobili and his Tamil counterparts in seventeenth-century South India, for instance. In these cases (and in Catholicism's post-Vatican II emphasis on inculturation) it is important to recognize both the instrumental nature of the processes and relationships of power that reify normatively Christian and non-Christian cultures as well as the agentive, dignifying, and religiously meaningful possibilities that inculturation creates for all involved.

Inculturation can also be related to the idea of enculturation, which is invoked a few times in this volume as well. In its classic formulations, enculturation (or socialization or acculturation) is the way a person comes to know and thereby reproduce cultural forms and norms; it is a technique for describing how cosmologies, values, taboos, linguistic codes, kinship patterns, expressive practices, and whatever else might fall under the catch-all "culture" are transmitted to children or non-native outsiders.[8] While the idea of enculturation seems to describe how the observable continuities and tangible differences that make "culture" something real come into being, its critics point out its reified, deterministic nature, its lack of nuance in addressing the relationship of structure and agency, and its ambivalence regarding change.

Bearing this in mind, there is, nevertheless, a shared, productive dimension to inculturation and enculturation. If inculturation is about the intercultural dynamics of religious translation and adaptation across differences, then enculturation can be about the intracultural dynamics of religious transmission and domestication within communities. In other words, enculturation can be understood as an extension of inculturation, the former being animated by charismatic "culture bearers" or in-group elites and the latter being animated by missionaries, evangelists, transnational religious formations, or states, for instance. While this approach does not circumvent the problem of "culture" latent in the ideas of inculturation and enculturation, it does move towards the kind of practice- and process-oriented approach I advocate at the end of this essay.

Meanings

Thinking, hearing, and writing in terms of inculturation bring ongoing debates in anthropology and ethnomusicology about the meaning of religious symbols and sounds to the fore. At the heart of these debates is a set of questions concerning the divergent theological, practical, and ethical approaches to inculturation: Is inculturation the expression of existing religious truths or the negotiation of new religious truths? Should religious practices be isomorphic across cultures or should they be similarly efficacious but formally different? Are similar practices the expressions of similar beliefs? To what extent is religious and cultural translation possible?

One approach to inculturation reflects the idea that meaning is transhistorical and inheres in or is embodied by religious symbols and sounds.[9] This kind of inculturation takes shape as a process of recontextualizing symbols and sounds within new or changing cultural conditions. Inculturation makes them meaningful by making them present, and isomorphism is taken as evidence of similar beliefs and efficacies. Another approach reflects the idea that meaning is enmeshed in social and historical particulars and is authorized collectively or institutionally through performance and repetition.[10] Symbols and sounds are meaningful because there is consensus or contestation, efficacy or failure. Here, recognition and resistance attest to the power that accrues to these religious symbols and sounds.

In this volume, both Hoffman and Tovey examine these different ways of producing meaning through the processes and practices of inculturation. For Hoffman, there is inculturation that shows and inculturation that explains, the former being inherently dialogic and more like the second approach I describe above, the latter being monolithic or potentially coercive and more like the first approach I describe above. For Tovey, following Victor Turner, there is inculturation based on the ideology of the symbol and inculturation based on the physical elements of the symbol, the former being an imposition and more like the first approach I describe above, the latter allowing for reinterpretation and more like the second approach I describe above.[11]

This constant concern with meaning in the practices and processes of inculturation is what reproduces religious orthodoxies and creates new syncretisms. However, inculturation conceived in terms of orthodoxy and syncretism depends upon ideological constructions of time and space. Inculturation becomes meaningful in relation to originary, authentic, legitimate times and places, which are normatively Western, or in relation to how those originary, authentic, legitimate meanings are transformed at a chronological or spatial distance, thereby becoming "local." So how might one think, listen, and write about inculturation beyond the "limits of meaning?"[12] How might one move, in Gregory Barz's words, "beyond syncretism towards consciousness?"[13]

One can move beyond the limits of inculturation-as-meaning and the derivative nature of syncretisms that posit more authentic, more integral opposites by thinking, listening, and writing about inculturation as performance, feeling, experience, consciousness, embodiment, and efficacy, for example. The essays in this volume dealing with inculturation model these possibilities in a number of ways: by describing the felt necessity of inculturation within communities of Eastern Christians living in the West, by embracing the new efficacies that inculturation creates as it redefines concepts of normalcy, health, illness, ability, and disability, and by reframing the project of inculturation as something fundamentally about Westerness and difference by focusing on forms of mediation within Western publics. To these models I will add a few specifically musical ones of my own in this final section.

Musical dynamics

Engaging the musical dynamics of inculturation necessitates moves beyond the limits of meaning because the ways in which inculturation happens musically are performative, feelingful, experiential, conscious, embodied, and efficacious. The musicality of inculturation reveals how new religious values, theologies, affective states, and modes of expression that deepen and elaborate canonical traditions come into being through the work of gifted individuals, the compulsion of rhythmic entrainment, the uncanniness of timbre, or the force of collective performance. The sounds of inculturation emerge in many ways — through the "baptism" of pre- or non-Christian genres and instruments, the rearrangement of forms and performance practices to meet practical liturgical needs, and the reimagination of musical ideals to better manifest the presence of the Holy Spirit, for instance. At the same time, listening to the sounds of inculturation — a brass band of Batak Christians in Sumatra playing their rendition of "Jesus, Keep Me Near The Cross"[14] or Orthodox Christians in Kodiak, Alaska, singing the tone seven "Lord I Call" in Yup'ik[15] — means questioning the relationship of emerging or long-established musical practices to religious orthodoxies.

So does the reproduction and performance of canonical religious sound bear witness to religious beliefs that are the same because of inculturation? Or do such practices give voice to new religious truths and beliefs, and suggest ways in which religious messages may become universal precisely because their expression is not syncretic or derivative but integral and full of agency? In other words, is the ontology of sacred sound — its revealed, prophetic, divine, and efficacious nature — translatable through inculturation, or are new ontologies of sacred sound engendered through inculturation?[16]

I suggest that the most valuable and illuminating answers to these questions come from ways of thinking, hearing, and writing about inculturation that neither collapse difference into sameness for the sake of orthodoxy, nor are content with the description of syncretism as the explanation of new religious phenomena. There is a third way of thinking, hearing, and writing about inculturation. This third way focuses more on the processes and practices of inculturation (and, by extension, enculturation) than on its outcomes; more on the negotiations, translations, and transformations that mediate religious messages in new cultural contexts and illuminate their value and potential in unexpected ways. Finally, this third way seeks out and takes seriously the experience and interpretation of those who have conventionally been subjects of inculturation—the colonized, the missionized, converts, minorities, non-Westerners, and those living in the global South. With this, we invert or move beyond the dynamics of inculturation, listening to and coming to understand religious, musical, and cultural change, personal transformation, and the making of theologies and soteriologies in the worlds of all those who practice world religions.

ENDNOTES

1. Also see C. Michael Hawn, "Singing with the Faithful of Every Time and Place: Thoughts on Liturgical Inculturation and Cross-Cultural Liturgy," *Colloquium: Music, Worship, Arts* 2 (2005): 109-24; and I-to Loh, "Contextualization versus Globalization: A Glimpse of Sounds and Symbols in Asian Worship," ibid., 125-39.

2. See, e.g., Richard Sobol and Jeffrey Summit, *Abayudaya: The Jews of Uganda* (New York: Abbeville Press, 2002).

3. "Introduction," *The Anthropology of Christianity*, ed. Fennella Cannell (Durham: Duke University Press, 2006), 26.

4. See, e.g., Peter van der Veer, ed., *Conversion to Modernities: The Globalization of Christianity* (New York: Routledge, 1996).

5. See, e.g., John Comaroff and Jean Comaroff, *Of Revelation and Revolution: Christianity, Colonialism, and Consciousness in South Africa*, 2 vols. (Chicago: University of Chicago Press, 1991-97); and John Bellarmine

Vallier, "Ethnomusicology as Tool for the Christian Missionary," *European Meetings in Ethnomusicology* 10 (2003): 85-97.

6. See, e.g., Philip Jenkins, *The New Faces of Christianity: Believing the Bible in the Global South* (New York: Oxford University Press, 2006).

7. See, e.g., Fennela Cannell, ed., *The Anthropology of Christianity* (Durham: Duke University Press, 2006); Simon Colemen, *The Globalization of Charismatic Christianity* (Cambridge: Cambridge University Press, 2000); and Joel Robbins, "On the Paradoxes of Global Pentecostalism and the Perils of Continuity Thinking," *Religion* 33 (2003): 221-31, and "The Globalization of Pentecostal and Charismatic Christianity," *Annual Review of Anthropology* 33 (2004): 117-43.

8. See Melville J. Herskovitz, *Man and His Works: The Science of Cultural Anthropology* (New York: Knopf, 1948), and *Acculturation: The Study of Culture Contact* (Gloucester, Mass.: P. Smith, 1958); Margaret Mead, "Socialization and Enculturation," *Current Anthropology* 4/2 (1963): 184-88; and Talcott Parsons and Robert F. Bales, *Family, Socialization, and Interaction Process* (Glencoe, Ill.: Free Press, 1955).

9. See Clifford Geertz, "Religion As a Cultural System," *The Interpretation of Cultures* (New York: Basic Books 2000 [1973]).

10. See Talal Asad, *Genealogies of Religion: Discipline and Reasons of Power in Christianity and Islam* (Baltimore: Johns Hopkins University Press, 1993).

11. Also see Phillip Tovey, *Inculturation of Christian Worship: Exploring the Eucharist* (Burlington, Vt.: Ashgate, 2004).

12. Matthew Engelke and Matt Tomlinson, eds., *The Limits of Meaning: Case Studies in the Anthropology of Christianity* (New York: Berghahn, 2006).

13. Gregory F. Barz, *Performing Religion: Negotiating Past and Present in Kwaya Music of Tanzania* (New York: Rodopi, 2003), 3.

14. Rob Boonzajer Flaes, *Brass Unbound: Secret Children of the Colonial Brass Band* (Amsterdam: Royal Tropical Institute, 2000).

15. *Beautiful Beyond: Christian Songs in Native Languages* (Smithsonian Folkways Recordings SFW40480, 2004).

16. See Philip V. Bohlman, "Ontologies of Music," in

Rethinking Music, ed. Nicholas Cook and Mark Everist (Oxford: Oxford University Press, 1999).

ADDITIONAL READING

Barz, Gregory F. "Soundscapes of Disaffection and Spirituality in Tanzanian *Kwaya* Music." *The World of Music* 47/1 (2005): 5-30.

— —. "'We are from different ethnic groups, but we live here as one family': The Musical Performance of Community in a Tanzanian *Kwaya*." In *Chorus and Community*, ed. Karen Ahlquist. Urbana: University of Illinois Press, 2006.

Garcia, Miguel A. "Conversión religiosa y cambio cultural." *Latin American Music Review* 19/2 (1998): 203-17.

Gray, Catherine. "Compositional Techniques in Roman Catholic Church Music in Uganda." *British Journal of Ethnomusicology* 4 (1995): 135-54.

Lange, Barbara Rose. *Holy Brotherhood: Romani Music in a Hungarian Pentecostal Church*. Oxford: Oxford University Press, 2003.

Lassiter, Luke Eric. "'From Here On, I Will Be Praying to You': Indian Churches, Kiowa Hymns, and Native American Christianity in Southwestern Oklahoma." *Ethnomusicology* 45/2 (2001): 338-52.

Mendoza, Zoila S. *Shaping Society through Dance: Mestizo Ritual Performance in the Peruvian Andes*. Chicago: University of Chicago Press, 2000.

Muller, Carol Ann. *Rituals of Fertility and the Sacrifice of Desire: Nazarite Women's Performance in South Africa*. Chicago: University of Chicago Press, 1999.

— —. "'Reading' the Book, Performing the Words of *Izihlabelelo zamaNazaretha*." *The World of Music* 47/1 (2005): 31-64.

Palackal, Joseph J. "Oktoechos of the Syrian Orthodox Churches in South India." *Ethnomusicology* 48/2 (2004): 229-50.

Poplawska, Marzanna. *The Role of Christian Music in the Processes of Inculturation and the Creation of Identity—an Indonesian Example*. Ph.D. diss., Wesleyan University, forthcoming.

Rappoport, Dana. "Ritual Music and Christianization in the Toraja Highlands, Sulawesi." *Ethnomusicology* 48/3 (2004): 378-404.

Romanowski, William D. "Evangelicals and Popular Music: The Contemporary Christian Music Industry." In *Religion and Popular Culture in America*, ed. Bruce David Forbes and Jeffrey H. Mahan. Berkeley: University of California Press, 2000.

Sarkissian, Margaret. "'Religion Never Had It So Good': Contemporary *Nasyid* and the Growth of Islamic Popular Music in Malaysia." *Yearbook for Traditional Music* 37 (2005): 124-52.

Scruggs, T. M. "(Re)Indigenization?: Post-Vatican II Catholic Ritual and 'Folk Masses' in Nicaragua." *The World of Music* 47/1 (2005): 91-124.

Sherinian, Zoe C. "Dalit Theology in Tamil Christian Folk Music: A Transformative Liturgy by James Theophilus Appavoo." In *Popular Christianity in India: Reading Between the Lines*, ed. Selva J. Raj and Corinne G. Dempsey. Albany: State University of New York Press, 2002.

— —. "The Indigenization of Tamil Christian Music: Musical Style and Liberation Theology." *The World of Music* 47/1 (2005): 125-65.

Spinney, Anne Morrison. "Medeolinuwok, Music, and Missionaries in Maine." In *Music in American Religious Experience*, ed. Philip V. Bohlman, Edith Blumhofer, and Maria Chow. Oxford: Oxford University Press, 2005.

Stillman, Amy Ku'uleialoha. "Prelude to a Comparative Investigation of Protestant Hymnody in Polynesia." *Yearbook for Traditional Music* 23 (1993): 89-99.

Jeffers Engelhardt is an ethnomusicologist whose research deals with music and religion, music, human rights, and cultural rights, and the musics of postsocialist Eurasia. He is currently the Andrew W. Mellon Visiting Assistant Professor of Music at Amherst College. He has published articles and reviews in the Yearbook for Traditional Music, The Journal of the Royal Anthropological Institute, Notes, *and* European Meetings in Ethnomusicology, *and has contributed chapters to several edited volumes. He is now at work on a book titled* Singing the Right Way: Renewal, Transition, and Orthodox Christianity in Estonia. *He holds a B.M. in Piano from the Oberlin Conservatory (1998) and an M.A (2000) and Ph.D. (2005) in Ethno-musicology from the University of Chicago. He is now at Amherst College as an assistant professor in the department of music.*

Ritual and Culture

Illness and Inculturation

LAWRENCE A. HOFFMAN

The Kavanagh Lecture delivered October 12, 2004

Envision this: I am visiting a hospital patient after massive brain surgery has left her temporarily (but maybe forever, everyone fears) unable to move or speak. Hearing of her illness, Debbie Friedman, a famous composer and singer of Jewish spiritual music, pays a surprise visit, guitar in hand. The patient somehow utters the Hebrew words *mi sheberakh*, the title of the Jewish prayer for healing, to which Debbie has written a now world-renowned melody. So Debbie sings it, and as she does, the patient unaccountably sings along, her first set of words in two weeks.

It is Christmas morning, as it happens, no special day for the patient, who is Jewish, but a significant occasion for her roommate, an elderly Haitian woman, who is surely not Jewish, but is clearly alone. Knowing spirit when she hears it, she joins in the chorus, garbled Hebrew and all. Through a mixture of song and tears, the patently morose room fills with modest sounds that cut across religion, class, culture, and race. We are all in need of healing and healing comes—through prayer.

Two years earlier, the same patient lies in bed, head attached to wires monitoring brain waves. Her roommate this time is an elderly African-American Pentecostal woman, a religious variety the patient has never before encountered. One Sunday, seven beautifully bedecked ladies visit, close the curtain, and pray up a storm. The Jewish patient—a college graduate who majored in Marxist thought (no less), so no automatic believer in a personal God—startles us with her question: "Why don't people pray like that for me?"

I am present both times because the patient is my daughter. I have prayed with her frequently outside the operating room, and again in recovery, wondering all the while why prayer means so much to someone who questions the whole enterprise of interceding with a personal deity.

My daughter is not alone. I have other instances too, like the story told by a rabbi who invites congregants with personal concerns to ascend to the ark, one by one, while Yom Kippur worship is progressing, and utter a silent prayer to God, as if each of them is alone rather than standing in front of a congregation of two thousand. When he sees his most outspoken congregational atheist standing in line for a turn, he is so surprised that he almost forgets to read the service. "I don't really believe in it," the atheist explains afterward, "but I just felt like doing it."

Why is that? Why does an outspoken religious cynic participate in a liturgy that puts him on public view as he accesses a God in whom he does not believe?

My theme here is the nexus of theology, liturgy, and illness—set in the context of inculturation, the most useful model, I have found, for the questions I have been forced to confront over nearly two decades of my daughter's chronic sickness.

A Genealogical Just-So

As a child raised in Canada, then proudly British enough to fly the Union Jack rather than a distinctively Canadian flag, I early came in contact with Rudyard Kipling's *Just-so Stories*: how the tiger got its stripes, the dog its growl, and the giraffe its neck. By extension, I now wonder how religion got its inculturation. My model, oddly, is Nietzsche's attack on Christian/Jewish ethics as a slave morality rooted in resentment (*ressentiment*) over the aristocratic values of the naturally superior.[1] *What* Nietzsche said is hardly what I champion, but I am in awe of *how* he said it: a literary technique so powerful that it is hard to forget his point even if we disagree with it: a philosophic genealogy, described by Bernard Williams as "a fictional narrative, an imagined developmental story, which helps to explain a concept or value or institution by showing ways in which it could come about." [2]

Nietzsche was not the first to discover the power of an argument set in fictitious history—philosophic genealogies go back to Plato, Locke, Rousseau, and Hume, whose imagined accounts of human history are equally attractive. Nor was he the last. Genealogies have figured prominently in recent accounts of such topics as knowledge, the state, and truthfulness. A genealogy is a particularly powerful "just so." [3]

Philosophical "just-so"s serve vital ends, as fancy often does. The physicist Vladimir Mlodinow, for instance, recalls imagining "a world with an infinite number of dimensions . . . up/down, right/left, and forward/backward, but also a countless array of other directions"—hardly the real thing of experience, but enough to spur a quantum leap into new ways of thinking that physicists now take for granted as true.[4] A quantum leap may be beyond my own personal reach here, but I do hope my imaginative history will help us rethink our pastoral theology and practice. I differentiate my tale from Kipling's just-so by renaming it "just-how," a genealogy describing "just how" inculturation was born.

Once upon a time, a tribe of prehistoric humans inhabited a land bordered on one side by a jungle and on the other by a lake or river (they didn't yet know the difference) where the opposite shore could be seen, though only barely, and only on clear days. Eventually, the spirit of discovery led the tribe to dispatch reconnaissance groups to see what lay within the jungle (not beyond it, of course, since they had as yet no notion of "beyondness"—the jungle, they fancied, went on forever). When the jungle actually ended at an ocean they reasonably concluded that they were at the end of the earth, warned against continuing further by the salty water that heaved up frightening waves when storms approached. So they returned home, but committed now to exploring the other direction, across the river, where they could, at least, see

an opposite coast. A second exploration party boarded rudimentary boats to see what lay there.

One of the party packed recipes for cooking native vegetables. Another memorized her grandmother's favorite lullaby. A police officer packed weapons. And, oh yes, there was also a rabbi (or priest, imam, pastor—substitute what word you will) who carried the sacred literature of his people, in part the tribal just-how story (just how the ancestors had met their gods in the first place), but also a just-what account (just what sacrifices, feasts, and fasts the gods expected of men and women). Some specialists brought the tribal rites, their music and performance that more or less acted out the just-how and the just-what. Thus were born theology and liturgy.

In the unlikely event of encountering other humanoids, the explorers reasoned, their gods just-might want to spread their own just-hows and just-whats among just-about-everyone.

The explorers found the opposite shore pretty much like their own: a little more rain, perhaps, and some slithery snakes they weren't too happy about, but they were pleased that their theologians had just-why explanations for these strange life forms—as they did for everything else. They also discovered sentient life not all that different from their own. It was the first time any single tribe had met another.

Now, one of the theologians in the landing party was named Pelikan. As it happens, a distant descendant of his, Jaroslav by name, was interviewed on National Public Radio on September 21, 2003, and asked to comment on space exploration. Intrigued by the possibility of sentience beyond humankind's latest river, outer space, Pelikan advised taking Bach's B Minor Mass, and beaming it as far as possible, with the message, "This is the best our species has done. Show us what you can do." More on Pelikan's advice later. This is not an argument for a classical cultural canon; it is just a philosophical genealogy that has reached its end so far in us. Human beings, we can conclude, are boat builders, who inherently like to show their best to others.

And that is "just how" inculturation got started: the human need to meet and greet no less than meet and beat, modified (to be sure) by such variables as power, greed, and theological certitude; and then, of late, modified back to counter those very same variables so as to avoid the imperialist hubris of the past. But inculturation is a two-way street. As it turns out, the second tribe too wondered if anyone lived across the river. When they discovered that the "anyone" not only existed, but was actually arriving in boats, they trotted out their own array of warriors, theologians, and liturgists, a curious but wary greeting party.

Only imperialists overlook the fact that the people on the other side of the river are equally certain of their gods and rites. Not having built boats first, they have never had to deal with the responsibilities of power, but they too have things to show. Inculturation is a dialogue between partners who beam their respective finest, and watch with bated breath to see what the other guys beam back. Inculturation is a case of mutual showing.

Inculturation is not just intercultural, however. It is inter-Other; it applies whenever some "one" meets some "other," as long as each party faithfully beams its stuff and watches for stuff being beamed back. It is inter-gender, for example, as long as men do not imagine that women are just men shaped differently—and vice versa. It is inter-class too—if, for instance, we were the tribe with the boats who chanced upon a society of billionaires, a case where our *Lex* meets their Lexus, so to speak, anomalous in the sense that the people being inculturated would be stronger than the inculturators.

My interest here, however, is illness. Visiting the sick is its own case of inculturation, an instance of mutual showing.

Illness as Territory

Suffering needs no genealogy. It comes with tales already written, like Tolstoy's *Death of Ivan Ilyich*. As cancer slowly saturates his body, Ivan becomes increasingly cut off from his usual haunts, his office especially. Illness becomes a virtual territory to which Ivan is banished. There, all alone, he suffers his decidedly unheroic death, much like that described hauntingly in Louise Harmon's *Fragments On the Deathwatch*.

> The mind—the thinking expressive remembering part of the human being—withdraws.... There is turning in toward the self, a curvature of the spine that directs the remaining life force toward the center. The knees of the dying human being are tucked up under the body. The arms are folded like a praying mantis, a caricature of moot supplication, and the petition is for safety.[5]

Thus do we all, eventually, shrink from sight, first to our own territory of the ill, and, eventually, into ourselves. After Ivan's death his erstwhile colleagues were sitting together when one of them, Peter Ivanovich (who was reading the newspaper) announced: "Gentlemen, Ivan Ilyich is dead." "I haven't seen him since the holidays," said Feydor Vasilievich. "I always meant to go, but he lived so terribly far away."[6]

Again, a geographic metaphor—the sick live far away—and it fits my genealogy, because it was a river that the boat builders had to cross, and it turns out that the reason Ivan lived "so terribly far away" is that his home was "on the other side of the river." Suppose Ivan's colleagues had crossed the river to visit. Could they have comprehended his ineffable torment? Those who have suffered chronic pain know that "for the person whose pain it is, [the pain] is 'effortlessly' grasped (that is, it cannot *not* be grasped); while for the person outside the sufferer's body, what is 'effortless' is [precisely] *not* grasping it."[7] The remarkable feature of pain is its victim's inability to express it. It is the sole internal state about which it can be said that the more frequent and extreme the suffering, the less likely anyone will believe the sufferer's claim that it is there.

To begin with, language utterly fails. "English," Virginia Woolf remarks, "which can express the thoughts of Hamlet and the tragedy of Lear has no words for a shiver or a headache. The merest schoolgirl, when she falls in love, has Shakespeare and Keats to speak her mind for her, but let a sufferer try to describe a pain in his head to a doctor, and language at once runs dry."[8]

Even worse, sickness becomes its own invisible culture, the "night-side of life," as Susan Sontag puts it. At birth, she says, we are issued two passports, one to the Land of the Well and the other to the Land of the Sick. We pocket the first and put aside the second, determined never to use it. But the day comes, for some of us earlier than others, when we must exchange passports, and when we do, we are, inexplicably and against our will, transported across a river to a land and culture not our own.[9] From time to time, brave boat builders (among whom we once lived) visit us, without realizing, however, that we are not the people we once were. Across the river we speak a language that only *sounds* the same as the language they still use.

By analogy, imagine a blind girl who encounters a seeing friend. Noticing that the girl is holding a playing board with white and black squares, the friend offers to join her in a game, promising, "Since you cannot see, I will move your pieces for you."

"Give me a standard opening," she replies, "two squares forward for the piece in front of the king."

"Standard?" asks her friend? "What's that? You don't get kings until the end of the game, and pieces move diagonally, a single square at a time."

A common game *board* does not insure a common *game*. The players here make sentences that parse in each other's mind, but they are talking two different languages, the language of chess and the language of checkers.

So too, citizens in the Land of the Sick only *seem* to talk the language of their visitors. The sicker they become, the more their meaning diverges, and the less the visitor gets what they are saying. Think through with me the phenomenon of conversation.

Our most elementary discourse is the white noise we use when we have nothing real to say.

"Hi, how are ya?"

"Fine thanks, and you?"

"Can't complain."

Elementary conversation is marked by this informational vacuity and shortness of duration, like, "It's raining again!" (as if that were not self-evident); or "Have a good one." These are instances of informationless chatter. "How are ya?" evokes "Fine thanks," because the question is not supposed to reveal the truth. It is a verbal handshake.

One level up is actual conversation, but usually about safe topics. It includes innocuous gossip:

"Did you hear what happened to Charlie?"

"No, what?"

"His wife left him!"

"No kidding!"

The content varies with culture and class, but for most readers of this journal I suspect it includes the news, movies, restaurants, and certainly our work and family. Most commonly heard is the plaint, "I'm *so* busy! I need a vacation."

These utterances too are ritualistic, in that acquiring information is less important than reaffirming human connection. It may be nice to know the name of the new restaurant, or the seamy details of Charlie's wife's latest love affair, but the point is less the data than the implication that the conversationalists share a social world: they can imagine going to the restaurant together; they have the same neighborly stake in Charlie and his wife.

Only at a third level do we get to issues of moment, politics (mostly) nowadays, religion once (when matters of faith mattered more). In either case we prefer discussions with people likely to agree with us, the point again being more social than informational. At a recent dinner a friend on my right was engaged in conversation with the woman on her right, who knew my opinion of some governmental policies, so assumed my friend felt similarly. "I work in health care," she said. "You won't believe what the White House is doing." "Actually," my friend replied, "my husband works for the President." The conversation was over. It was a conversational foray that failed, an aborted ritual of dinner companionship.

When we really want information we structure conversation at a fourth level up, in impersonal gatherings called meetings, classes, or lectures. Since its purpose isn't social, we limit it not to friends (as at dinner parties), but to an impersonal list of official "members" who may not know each other and may not want to, or to anonymous fee-payers who buy the right to hear intellectual property.

There is, however, yet a fifth level of informational conversation, where, just the opposite, only our nearest and dearest get invited in: discussion of our bodies, the most intimate thing we have. To the outside world, we keep our bodies hidden. Ugly scars are covered. Makeup masks the face, as deodorant does our smell. Only family and close friends dare ask if our athlete's foot or urinary infection has improved.

Almost the only thing that matters in the Land of the Sick is body talk, the very conversation that the Land of the Well avoids. If you have chronic Crone's disease or must wear a permanent catheter what counts is *precisely*, and, on many days, *only* your digestive or urinary tract. For the sick, says Arthur Kleinman in his *Illness Narratives*, "Details [of the body] are all ... [C]hronic illness means ... routinely scan[ning] minute bodily processes ... sometimes hour by hour." As sports buffs can describe any single

pass in a football game with sufficient poetic grace to differentiate it from any other pass, so the chronically ill specialize in the fine art of defining the uniqueness of a headache or back pain on any given day, an art they practice, despite the limits of language, endlessly — since "symptoms must be explained [again and again] to receptionists, nurses, doctors," and there is always the question of just how and how much to say to friends and colleagues.[10]

Take Pat, who became a victim of scleroderma, an auto-immune disorder that calcifies internal organs, sometimes causing early death. When early symptoms persisted, she visited, in succession, her family doctor, an internist, a dermatologist, a neurologist, an allergist, and a cardiologist. Along the way she had an electroneurograph, electrocardiogram, and venogram — two of which she had never heard of before.[11] The sick become learned in the specialized vocabulary of anatomy, and the intricacies of medical care, to the point where they may be virtually unable to abide the ordinary conversation from the Land of the Well.

Honest ritualized conversation with the sick would go like this:

"How are you?" "Awful, I may be dying."

"Have a good one!" "Are you kidding?"

"Hear about the new restaurant opening in town?" "No, but there's a new nursing home on Shady Lane."

"I am so busy at work." "I'm so busy lying in hospital beds, waiting."

"I wish I had a vacation." "*I* wish I could work!"

Philosophically, the issue is both intentional and lexical. By "intentional" I mean that utterances come with assumed states of mind that determine their conditions of satisfaction.[12] "How are you?" is not normally a request for data. But people dying (sometimes, literally) to provide information that might otherwise be called for will find the normal response ("Fine, thank you") unsatisfying. By "lexical" I mean that conversation is peppered with strange terms.

"I'm in for a vesico-vaginal fistula—that's a breakdown of communication between the bladder and the wall of the vagina."

"Really! Hmmm. They caught *my* problem with a hepatoboliary scan whereby a nuclear camera traces radioactive dye in my gallbladder."

This is not dinner conversation; but if chronic conditions persist, they are what you naturally think about—all the time. Regular doctor's appointments and their inevitable medical regimens mean seeing fewer movies; dietary limitations make party-going difficult; with fewer conversations to affirm companionship, you become companionless—except among the other sick. Old friends stop crossing the river to visit because they don't know what to say, or, if they do some day drop anchor, they say what the sick cannot hear, and hear what the sick are not saying. How do we bring religious promise to people who speak a different language from our own? How do we cross the river, and what do we beam to them when we get there? Our interactive competence is limited by our own life space, what Pierre Bourdieu calls *habitus*, meaning "a feel for the game."[13] Inculturation as "encounter with another" consists of being thrown into altogether new games and trying to get a feel for them.

As I said, I have been thrown into such a game. I understand why its favored metaphor is military. A virus *invades*; we get heart *attacks*; illnesses *advance* like threatening armies. A hospital has an *operating* room; the Pentagon has one for *operations*. I live under *siege*, each day renewing the battle, and worried that my daughter, sick now for twenty years, is losing the war. I visit her in the hospital, her home away from home as she calls it (joking that she will some day write a *Zagat's* Guide to Hospitals, rating them in number of beds, not stars), and discover to my horror that even I am sometimes on the other side of the river, her shore receding more and more even as I think I am landing there. She is within arm's length, but as she worsens, she thinks increasingly differently than she did, and

I, becoming one with her, speak increasingly differently than my colleagues and friends. I watch well-meaning visitors have non-conversations with her. I ferry back and forth from shore to shore, on one side hospital and sickness, on the other the *New York Times* with all the news that's fit to print but increasingly uninteresting.

Irving Goffman differentiates the metaphorical *front* room of our lives, where we greet clients, parishioners, customers, and strangers, from the *back* room where only those we trust are granted admission to see us as we really are—mistakes, messiness, and all. I have become a backroom hospital dweller. I warm up food in the nurses' station; I welcome new patients to their rooms as if I were a volunteer at immigration, helping them unpack their suitcase of sorrows. The hospital cafeteria has become my office where I joke with cashiers, banter with security, meet with students, and write this article.

I am struck also by my own back room at home: a study in creeping entropy: multiple medicine schedules with the complexity of spread sheets, and pill bottles scattered on the bathroom counter. On the floor are varieties of ear plugs, new and used, that my daughter wears to deaden sounds that trigger seizures; also trays for eating in bed; heating pads and cold compresses too. The fallout of illness crowds out everything.

This material detritus is an iconic reminder of a deeper dislocation: the interruption of a life narrative. I include here the many others who end up across the river: parents of children born with terrible disabilities, perhaps, or who lose a child and never quite recover. Chronic pain syndrome is especially alienating. Family members leave, divorce, or disappear, and even your own doctors begin judging you a nuisance. Each variety of illness has its own vast literature of sorrow. But one thing they share is the need to remake one's life story.

Life stories are central to culture. Americans notice birthdays, anniversaries, graduations, and first-time things like first words, first steps, first date, and first kiss—happy firsts, note, not first family funeral, for instance. What causes the sick special difficulty is the fact that ours is a culture of celebration. We take pictures at weddings (again, not funerals), then arrange them with life's other happy landmarks in photo albums or on walls: "That was me as a baby; there I am getting married; here I am bringing you home from the hospital when you were just born; and there you are at first communion," a mother instructs her child. We expect the young to dream a future; the aged to revisit their past; the middle aged to have (and to overcome) mid-life crises. At death, their story is canonized in an official eulogy.

Like everyone else, chronically ill people too start out with hopeful dreams and diary, but illness makes them revisionist historians. As I clean out my daughter's room, I find piles of essays she once wrote, soccer trophies she once won, the French horn music she never could play very well, letters from friends she once had, and magazines she used to be able to read. She glances through them on occasion, but mostly they are detritus now, decomposing with time. Who, then, is she? What is her story? How will she be remembered, if stages of her illness become also her life cycle; if hospital stays supplant birthdays as time's lasting landmarks?

For people in chronic distress, our sacred calendars and their liturgies lose credibility, because they reflect only the lives of the healthy. The chaplain makes a call, but then goes home for a real Christmas dinner, while the hospital food-service brings the patient an *ersatz* variety to eat alone in bed. It comes with a well-intentioned but mechanically produced card in red and green, saying, "Merry Christmas." Similarly, "Shabbat shalom" says the rabbi, as a matter of habit; or, on Rosh Hashanah, "May you be inscribed for a good year." Sure! For some, religion offers theological models of suffering and of hope; I do not make light of that. The lucky ones do find meaning in their malady. But for many our promise is pat; our words troubling.

The Talmud reports a rabbi who tells a grieving father that his sins may have been visited on his son. "You came to comfort him but you only made things worse!" the Talmud charges (Ket. 8b). How can we ensure that we are not similarly guilty, because of what we say? What exactly *do* we bring with us across the river?

Theology and Liturgy: What We Bring with Us

I find myself returning again and again to Clifford Geertz's threefold typology of what I will call limit points in human experience: "intellectual bafflement, inexplicable suffering, and ethical paradox." His typology is worth pausing over because it relates precisely to what Geertz assumes religion provides: meaning. He is not alone in that demand—the claim that religion provides meaning goes back at least to Weber, and has been accepted under one rubric or another ever since. Geertz usefully contrasts the Weberian view with Benthamite utilitarianism: not happiness but meaning is the ultimate ideal of human life, to which "ignorance, pain and injustice" are said to be the primary impediments.[14]

I could add other breaking points too: aesthetic wonder, for example, and physical endurance. Geertz might equally have claimed that aesthetics is akin to order, that (with Mary Douglas) "matter out of place" is "dirt," and that the pervasive sense of disorder is equally inimical to cultural meaning; or that it need not take actual bodily pain to occasion meaninglessness—poor physical stamina, as is experienced regularly with a chronic illness like lupus, will do it with equal effectiveness.

It would appear that human striving beyond known limits is the cultural antidote to our fear of failure at the breaking points. Scientific inquiry, medical advance, artistic expression, athletic performance, and so forth, continually demonstrate the human ability to stretch our limits—as when Roger Bannister first broke the four-minute mile, something we all take for granted now, making successively new records the latest unbelievable feat to beat; or when mathematicians solve problems that have proven intractable for centuries. Even our ability to endure suffering can increase with effort—a twisted parallel, perhaps, to a runner's personal best. Some religious personalities—like medieval saints who consciously sought pain—have deliberately approached suffering as a form of embodied spiritual discipline; and, indeed, athletes too sometimes measure success by the pain they are able to endure ("No pain, no gain," as the saying goes).

But ethical paradox differs. It is the single limit point that defies progress, changing not one whit from the classical biblical statement by Job. Suffering may indeed be something we learn to master, but, even if we do, we want it at least to be ethically defendable; it should have purpose, demonstrate nobility, represent sacrifice for a greater cause, be our just desserts as punishment for sin, or constitute part of a larger divine plan. We thereby hope to rescue pain from being "inexplicable," as Geertz calls it.

When I say that pain should be ethically defendable, I speak from the vantage point of the victim, not the oppressor. I may undergo torture rather than be false to my faith, but torture remains an evil. It may have "made sense" for the civil rights workers of the 1950s to know they were being beaten for the cause of freedom, but their beating was not on that account an ethical act being inflicted upon them. At stake is the subjective judgment of the sufferer who wants to know her suffering is not in vain.

We see now that Bentham and Weber are not altogether at odds with each other. To the extent that we find any of the breaking points meaningful, we mitigate their pain. Suffering occasioned by sickness takes us first to physicians who, we hope, will remove the suffering. When that fails, the next logical step is to live with the pain through normal, and, if necessary, abnormal analgesics. And when that fails, we turn to religion in the hope of making our suffering

meaningful. If religion cannot end suffering, it should at least make suffering sufferable. It should, that is, have meaning.

Or should it?

That depends on what we mean by meaning. Nowadays, the search for meaning is endemic, but what complicates matters is the ongoing disagreement on the meaning of meaning among those who think about how we think. That very title ("The Meaning of Meaning") was featured in a series of articles in the celebrated philosophical journal *Mind*, beginning in April, 1920, and was reported on in a book by the same name in 1923. The authors of the latter cite a description of the symposium six months later (April, 1921) as "a triangular duel, in which each participant aims at something different, and, according to the other, misses it."[15] The meaning of "meaning" is far from obvious.

The word is much used, but differently, depending on context. There is psychological meaning behind behavior, hermeneutical meaning of texts, philosophical meaning of language, authorial meaning in literature, artistic meaning of film, semiological meaning in dress codes, and even romantic meaning as in, "Our relationship is, like, you know, just so, like, *meaningful*!" Does everything have meaning, even sickness? And if so, what meaning does it have?

For my purposes, I am content to look for what Charles Taylor calls "Experiential Meaning," by which he means "the meaning of something in a field," as opposed to linguistic meaning, which adds the variable of "signifiers in a world of referents."[16] We want to know what subjective meaning illness has for the people who suffer it: the coherent explication of a victim's suffering by the victim, and intended as edification of what this suffering is "all about." In part it is purely subjective, deriving from the victim's own imagination; but in part it is cultural, since meaning exists only "in a field," and the field is the repertoire of potential explanations that society makes available.

In this experiential sense, sickness

obviously embeds *some* meaning—"symptomatic meaning," for instance. In the Land of the Well a headache implies a traffic jam getting to work, or two kids at home with ear infections. In the Land of the Sick it may mean a brain tumor returning. As revisionist historians, patients also search for "narratival meaning," the integration of sickness into their ongoing biography.[17] But neither of these is the kind of meaning that Weber intended. People who suffer want to know that their pain has the kind of *moral* meaning that responds to the transcendent question, "Why?"[18]

That is where theologians come in, for if theology does not supply the field of transcendent meanings, what does? The sick approach theology, therefore, as if it were the medicine of meaning, for which pastors are the doctors, the meaning-makers. But the analogy fails. In medicine, patients need not really understand their diagnosis: they simply deliver themselves up for prescribed procedures like MRIs and blood tests, after which they memorize the results as litanies to rehearse for the inquisitive, even if what they memorize doesn't actually signify anything. It simply feels satisfying to know we suffer from *something* rather than *nothing*, even "idiopathogenesis," which is to say, an "idiopathic condition of unknown etiology," which translates further as "a primary disease, but we don't know what it is or what caused it."

The visiting pastor, by contrast, cannot mask absence of meaning in leftover Greek and Latin. She is more akin to a traveling sales representative, selling theological meaning in words that work only because patients internalize them as their own. Having a theological claim that coheres with the rest of the patient's world view is the very essence of experiential meaning. They are sinners, perhaps; or the objects of God's inscrutable but benevolent will; Jesus suffered pain; God tries people; the Lord is our shepherd; we all die sooner or later. But given the language gap between the two lands, how do we know that what we say is what the patient gets? "God's in-scrutable will" may just be theological idiopathogenesis. What in the world are we doing when we speak of God's mercy, blessing, hope; or when we say "hallowed be thy name" in a land where words *sound* the same but *mean* differently?

The *search* for meaning may be ubiquitous; its *existence* may not. Stanley Fish describes preparing for class by erasing the chalkboard notes of a prior lecturer, but halfway through being called away for a conversation. Upon returning, he finds his students taking notes on the random list of words remaining on the board, and filling in the logical gaps to make the list mean an outline of what they assume Fish will teach.[19]

Fish's class suggests the schizophrenics described by Annie Dillard.[20] She gives us the psychologist Hans Prinzhorn who finds meaning in the notes that schizophrenics make about random patterns in raindrops, but who can legitimately do so only if the meanings that schizophrenics find are not really there. Do the schizophrenics properly take notes on their raindrops, or does Dr. Prinzhorn properly take notes on their notes? They can't both be right. Are our theological notes on illness more like schizophrenics' notes on raindrops or like psychological notes on the schizophrenics' notes? Some things may have *no* transcendent meaning, none, at least, that outsiders may rightfully impute to them. By analogy, Susan Sontag thinks art is not necessarily *about* anything; it just *is*. Art critics "should … *show* … that it is what it is, rather than what it means." Art interpretation, she complains, tames what it interprets.[21]

Theologians, we trust, are not schizophrenics, finding something in nothing. But we are also not scientists explicating objective demonstrables. When it comes to illness, we are like art critics, charged with *showing* that suffering is what it is, not *taming* it by assigning it moral meaning.

So we are back at *showing*—showing the art of artistry (for Sontag), showing Bach's B Minor Mass (for Pelikan), and showing whatever it was that the theologians of my genealogy brought with them. The proper role of theologians who visit the Land of the Sick is to facilitate the showing of suffering. But in *inculturational* showing, we saw, the one showing and the one being shown trade roles. Conquering colonialists were apt to show their wares and kill you if you didn't buy them. Inculturation is the trading of shows by equals.

My best example, though not the most delicate, is the childhood discovery of sex, in a game called, "I'll show you, if you show me." For the game to work, the players must be freely consenting equals—if, say, by contrast, it is an adult "playing" with a child, we call it sexual abuse; and the two players must agree on a prior understanding of what counts as a proper showing.

So: from children's sex to Pelikan's Bach. What could Pelikan's extraterrestrial creatures have made of Bach, were they not also to share curiosity about an agreed-upon category of what counts as showing? How do the extraterrestrials know it is music? Or culture? And *not*, say, sex? Showing is a game with *rules* about what *counts* as a *show*.

We have reached the point, then, where the Lands of the Well and of the Sick may enter into inculturational dialogue, but by *showing*, not *explaining*. Discursive conversation is likely to resemble my chess/checker example, where identical verbal moves mean different things. "The meek shall inherit the earth," the pastor says. "I see," answers the patient, dubiously, thinking, "Go on. But I doubt it."

Ludwig Wittgenstein correctly remarks, "Certain things cannot be put into words... [they] make themselves manifest. They are what is."[22] They arise from the narrative truths of one's own life. I count suffering among them. Wittgenstein imagines a religious person who says illness is divine punishment, a proposition he, Wittgenstein, would deny, but not the way he would deny a claim that a friend was in town on a certain day. In the latter case he would look for common evidence that confirms or denies the picture of her being there. In the religious instance, says Wittgenstein, "I think differently. I say different things to myself. I have different *pictures*."[23] *Pictures*, note. What are *pictures*, if not *showing*?[24]

Now you know why my genealogy included a liturgist. Liturgy is the medium of theological showing: processing with the Bible; singing a chorale; witnessing at prayer; raising high a Torah scroll. Even telling our sacred story. For stories are words that "show"—the Israelites leaving Egypt, Christ on the cross. One of the most substantive changes of our time is the personalization of liturgical participation generally, but especially here, where the sick can speak their own piece,[25] tell their own stories, show their own experience.[26] Imagine a photographer taking a picture of someone who objects, "That's not me; it doesn't do me justice." Failing vanity, we should trust the subject; it probably doesn't. Liturgy must learn to listen to the stories of those present, and to change what it says if the standard liturgical picture does not do justice.

I am arguing against two common misunderstandings of liturgical communication: liturgy as description, and prayer as petition. As to the first, since showing is not describing, it can hardly be identified as a set of declarative sentences that mirror actual states of affairs. "God is our help," and "Angels surround a throne of glory," for instance, are not the same kinds of claims as a hospital patient saying, "My nurse is my help," or a historian claiming, "In the palace of Louis XVI, courtiers surrounded the king's throne of glory." As to petition, it may seem that our liturgies evoke divine help, but such entreaties are not the same as requests to a librarian to supply a stipulated book from the stacks, or to a doctor to provide a cure. Requesting God's pardon differs from asking pardon from another motorist after scraping the bumper of his car; or (different yet) requesting pardon from the court; or even (different yet again) saying "Pardon me" after a sneeze. Language is always dependent on context, and, as we saw with Wittgenstein's example, ordinary language applied to religion is especially deceiving.[27] The word "believe," for example, in "I believe it will rain today," may be innocent elevator chatter or part of a staged debate among experts on the weather channel. "I believe God exists," however, is a normative announcement of moral virtue.[28] The difference is more readily apparent if we consider their negations. "I don't believe it will rain" is equally innocent, while "I don't believe in God" raises serious eyebrows. "Ya gotta believe" may be a rule governing membership in a religious group or the prerequisite for being saved, but it can also be a baseball cheer for the New York Mets. Liturgical language always runs into difficulties when it is misunderstood as belonging to the canons of ordinary talk about the world.

I said before, and I grant again now, that many sick people do find the declarative claims of theology morally compelling. They accept their identity as God's "suffering servant," "a sufferer in Christ," or whatever other model we offer.[29] But my topic, remember, is people in pain who find those claims uncompelling, but who find prayer appealing anyway and wonder why. At stake is how we judge liturgy's relevance. If prayers for the sick are primarily petitionary, they should answer to criteria of efficacy, a test that they regularly fail.

Yet what compels the participation even of skeptics in their moments of agony seems to be precisely prayer's *petitionary* nature. With doctors failing, maybe God really will decide to intervene. It is that rationale that has prompted experiments to demonstrate that God hears prayer. Wayne Dossey, for example, cites the research of Randolph Byrd. Byrd lists the names of patients suffering a given malady, and assigns half the list to anonymous others who agree to pray for them without their knowing it. The other half goes unprayed-over. The prayed-over, he contends, were (among other things) five times less likely to require antibiotics; also (though the difference here is statistically insignificant) fewer of them died. The claim has been refuted by further research,[30] but, for the sake of argument,

suppose we grant its veracity, and even extend it. Imagine that sixty percent of the prayed-over, but only forty percent of the unprayed-over, got better. What should we conclude?

The experiment is plagued with problems, not the least being the moral one of deliberately withholding prayer from fifty percent of a population when you hypothesize in advance that they are more likely to worsen or die as a result.[31] But more to the point here, the science of the experiment is worthless. For one thing, nearly everyone nowadays knows someone who knows someone who prays over them. Who knows who gets prayer and who doesn't? The most Dossey can conclude is that God hears the prayers of certain worshipers more than others, and I suspect Dossey would agree with this conclusion. We ought, anyway, to suspect scientists who demonstrate God's existence by demonstrating how prayer is answered, but conclude their report by thanking God for demonstrating that their demonstration is right.

Most of all, there is the crying theological need to explain the people who did not get better. First, the unprayed-over: does God abandon poor souls just because they have no one to pray over them? And what about the forty percent of those who got prayed over but who continued suffering anyway? Should they decide, with Job's "comforters," that they deserve their suffering — and therefore suffer doubly, first through illness, then through guilt? Or is this the inscrutable will of God who whimsically heals one righteous patient but not another?

I cannot say if, when, why, or how prayer is efficacious in Dossey's terms — no one can — but I consider the whole issue liturgically irrelevant. Prayer as petition is a reasonable and justifiable mode of conduct even for people who suspect that God will *not* intervene for them. Quintessential cynics who find theological discussion maddening, but repeatedly pray to a God in whom they do not believe, are not just muddled liturgical recidivists — people so naturally habituated to prayer that they repeatedly return to it.

No longer Aristotelian scientists, we need not hold that as rocks fall to earth because of the nature of rockiness, humans pray because of the nature of humanness. True, all animals ritualize, and we are animals. Still, all animals seek food too, but only because food nourishes them. How then does petition as *ritual* nourish, even when petition as *petition* fails?

Ritual is not systematic theology. In prayer as *ritual* the cognitive content, whether descriptive or petitionary, matters relatively little. The normative process by which watchdog committees scan liturgical scripts for theological precision is wrongheaded. People who attend liturgies may not even be able to tell you what the liturgies said. They will often have recited (or, certainly, sung) propositions they do not believe—though they do not exactly disbelieve them either: the liturgical language game is not about belief and disbelief. A Jewish atheist who avoids God-sentences in normal conversation will nonetheless recite, "Hear O Israel, the Lord our God the Lord is One,"[32] and will petition God without expecting the petition to be granted. Because it is a ritual, liturgy functions best when it is not presented primarily as didactic information that must be pondered in order to be granted cognitive acceptance. A very great deal of it conveys predictable (because invariant) givens. Of necessity, the mode of liturgical communication renders a prayer's manifest content relatively inconsequential.

Freud was on to this as early as 1911, when he famously likened worship's seemingly mindless repetitiveness to obsessive-compulsive behavior, an idea he would later pursue in detail in his celebrated *Totem and Taboo*. His critique was taken up by others, who were hardly Freudians, but who drew on information theory to demonstrate the cognitive vacuity of liturgical speech. Amount of information is said to vary inversely with the extent to which one can predict what will be said. To the extent that liturgies are predictable, they say nothing at all; and to the extent that they say nothing at all, they preclude refutation. No one rises to object, "Hear O Israel, the Lord our God may not exist."

Neo-Marxists condemn liturgy for its deliberate use of redundancy to obfuscate, but Durkheimians applaud it for the very same thing: its "chants, song, dance, music, [and] verbal formulas" that make the communication compelling,[33] and its ability to provide undeniable canonical truths on which believers stake their lives.[34]

Both sides are right. Ritual's relative dearth of content makes it heavenly or diabolic, but in either case effective. It allows us to say what we otherwise do not believe. Prayer is like a commentary to museum retrospectives, like program notes to a great symphony, like a tourist's guidebook. These things do not *say* anything so much as *show* what is going on, lending appreciation to an otherwise enigmatic canvass by Jackson Pollack, the revolutionary genius of Beethoven, or the various arches of the El-Aksa Mosque. Pain, suffering, grief—these have no moral meaning; they have only grave reality, that rites of healing may at best elucidate, in language that only *sounds* descriptive or petitionary.

In the end, then, liturgy becomes photography, which was the medium par excellence to awaken the world to the reality of suffering. Photography was invented in 1839, and came of age precisely when wars increased in ferocity undreamed of earlier: the generalized use of gunpowder in the Civil War, machine guns for the Crimean War (1854-56), and trench warfare of World War I. In just the Battle of the Somme, sixty thousand British troops alone died or were severely wounded in the very first day, thirty thousand of them in the first half hour. In the next four and a half months, the number would rise to one million three hundred thousand as the line of combat moved only five miles. That is two hundred sixty thousand bodies or parts thereof per mile, one hundred forty-eight bodies per yard, forty-nine bodies per foot. A "mere" five hundred fifty thousand died in Ypres, but pieces of bodies were still being unearthed

eighty-five years later in 2003.[35] The master
essayist Henry James, who lived through those
days, declared stunningly, "War has used up
words." What could not be expressed, even by
James, could be shown in photographs precisely
because, said Virginia Woolf, another eye-wit-
ness of the time, photographs "are not an
argument, [but] simply a crude statement of fact
addressed to the eye." Where pain and suffering
abound, that is all we have: not arguments, but
imagery.[36]

In the end, then, theology meets sickness
by a mutual beaming back and forth, just what
Pelikan described. You can't explain the B Minor
Mass to extraterrestrials; you just play it, and
hope they will play something back. Prayer is "on
the spot" photography of ultimate human dilem-
mas. Its very power lies in the fact that, posing
no question, it pretends to no answer. The most
ardent skeptic can dispense with argumenta-
tion—and just watch the picture.

Such "liturgy-that-shows" honors the sick
whose lives we otherwise would be invading with
self-righteous religious rhetoric, no different in
kind than when the colonial powers brought the
good news to natives without regard for what
the natives had to say in return. It allows us to
resist the temptation to describe, explain, or at-
tribute moral meaning to what we do not know
ourselves first-hand.

Prayer is not description (despite its
descriptive language) nor is it petition (despite
its patent requests). No theological world need
correspond to the descriptions we give, and no
supernatural power need respond to the requests
we make. Liturgy is ritualized redundancy that
lets us show what ordinary conversation pre-
cludes, and lets liturgical writers be open to what
liturgical participants show in return.

ENDNOTES

1. "It was the Jews who, in opposition to the aristocratic
equation (good = aristocratic = beautiful = happy
= loved by the gods), dared with a terrifying logic to
suggest the contrary equation, and indeed to maintain
with the teeth of the most profound hatred (the
hatred of weakness) this contrary equation, namely,
'the wretched are alone the good; the poor, the weak,
the lowly, are alone the good; the suffering, the needy,
the sick, the loathsome, are the only ones who are
pious, the only ones who are blessed, for them alone is
salvation …'" (Friedrich Nietzshe, *Beyond Good and
Evil*, 1.7, trans. Horace B. Samuel, in *The Philosophy of
Nietzsche* [The Modern Library; New York: Random
House, 1927], 643).

2. Bernard Williams, *Truth and Truthfulness* (Princeton: Princeton University Press, 2002), 31.

3. Besides Williams see, e.g., Robert Nozick, *Anarchy,
State, and Utopia* (New York: Basic Books, 1974), and
E. J. Craig, *Knowledge and the State of Nature* (Oxford:
Clarendon Press, 1990).

4. Leonard Mlodinow, *Feynman's Rainbow* (New York:
Warner Books, 2003), 4. A genealogy is "an explanation
that would be correct if everythingz in it were true and
operated" (Williams, *Truth*, 31). In Mlodinow's case,
what he imagines is potentially true and operative in
another world, such that thinking it to be so allowed
him to "show how certain problems in atomic physics
would be easily solvable *if* the world had an infinite
number of dimensions." The point is that he "eventually showed how to compensate for the false assumption of infinite dimensions, and find answers that are
accurate and relevant to our three-dimensional world"
(Mlodinow, 40).

5. Louise Harmon, *Fragments on the Deathwatch* (Boston: Beacon Press, 1998), 7.

6. Leo Tolstoy, *The Death of Ivan Ilyich*, opening dialogue (abridged).

7. Elaine Scarry, *The Body in Pain* (Oxford: Oxford
University Press, 1985), 4.

8. Virginia Woolf, "On Being Ill," in *Collected Essays* 4
(New York: Harcourt, 1967), 194. Cited in Scarry, 4.

9. Susan Sontag, *Illness as Metaphor and AIDS and Its
Metaphors* (New York: Anchor Books, 1990), 3.

10. Arthur Kleinman, *The Illness Narratives: Suffering,
Healing, and the Human Condition* (New York: Basic
Books. 1988), 47, 45, 48.

11. See Henry Scammell, *Scleroderma* (New York: Evans and Company, 2003), 37-50.

12. See John Searle, *Minds, Brains, and Science* (Cambridge: Harvard University Press, 1984), 57-70.

13. Pierre Bourdieu, *Practical Reason: On the Theory of Action* (Stanford: Stanford University Press, 1998), 25.

14. Clifford Geertz, *Interpretation of Cultures* (New York: Basic Books, 1973), 100, 108. On making suffering sufferable, see p. 104.

15. C. K. Ogden and I. A. Richards, *The Meaning of Meaning* (1923; London: Ark Paperbacks, 1985), 161.

16. Charles Taylor, "Interpretation and the Sciences of Man," in his *Philosophy and the Human Sciences* (Cambridge: Cambridge University Press, 1985), 23.

17. Kleinman (*The Illness Narratives*) identifies four meanings: (1) what symptoms mean in terms of illness, what he calls "the surface meaning" (e.g., "Recurring back pain means the return of cancer"); (2) the social meanings of illness that society delivers to the sick (e.g., "AIDS denotes immoral behavior"); (3) the meanings from their prior life that the sick project upon their own illness (e.g., "I always knew I would die of cancer; it is just my family's fate"); and (4) the meanings illness has for the ongoing narrative of a sick person's life (e.g., "I was wrong to aspire to become a doctor; but I can still do good by bearing witness to the world's pain").

18. See Charles Taylor, "Interpretation," 27.

19. Stanley Fish, *Is There a Text in This Class?* (Cambridge: Harvard University Press, 1980), 322-23.

20. Annie Dillard, *Living By Fiction* (New York: Harper and Rowe, 1982), 137-38.

21. Susan Sontag, *Against Interpretation and Other Essays,* (New York, Picador Books, 1961).

22. Ludwig Wittgenstein, *Tractatus Logico-Philosophicus,* revised ed. (London: Routledge and Kegan Paul, 1974), 6:522.

23. Cyril Barrett, ed., *Lectures and Conversations on Aesthetics, Psychology, and Religious Belief [by] L. Wittgenstein. Compiled from Notes taken by Yorick Smythies, Rush Rhees, and James Taylor* (Berkeley: University of California Press, 1967), 167. The same issue is broached in a different way in his *On Certainty* (ed. G. E. M. Anscombe and G. H. Wright; trans. Denis Paul and G.

E. M. Anscombe [New York: Harper Torchbook, 1972]). "Doubting the existence of the external world [the idealists' issue] does not mean, for example, doubting the existence of a planet, which later observations proved to exist" (# 20). Doubt (and, therefore, certainty) depends on the rule that governs use, and, therefore, "What could a mistake here be like?" (#51). Take Moore's celebrated holding of his hands aloft to "show" [prove?] that, contra idealism, existence is real. Then, "Of course he may be wrong about this," but "what is it like to make such a mistake as that?" (#32). We know when we have gone wrong only because someone who knows the rule says, "This, and what is pointed to here is something indeterminate" (#28). We know we go wrong when someone who knows the rule shows us what is wrong. Showing is beyond telling. Telling depends on showing.

It seems to me that Wittgenstein's case of showing as "mystical" is another instance of the same thing: getting at something that can only be shown but not said. Mystics manage to say a great deal about their subject, but its appreciation requires the experience of knowing it first hand—as if a mystic puts us in a trance and says, "See!," thereby showing us what all the words mean.

24. This example (and others) are discussed in greater detail with regard to ritual, generally, as showing in my "A Rendezvous of Ancestors: Wrestling for Ritual Truth," *Proceedings of the North American Academy of Liturgy* (2004): 26-31.

25. In a colonial era bearing witness consists of the people we conquer admitting the truths of the conquerors. Inculturation instructs us that as much as our language can become theirs, they can and do alter our language.

26. Liturgical scripts can be open or closed. Pre-inculturation liturgies are closed. We tell people what to say. Inculturated liturgies are open. There is a place for people to say their piece—in their own words. What they say is incorporated into our liturgical language, for their words show what they alone know, and when we meet others more similar to them than to us we need to be able to modify "our showing" by "theirs."

27. Word-meaning is governed by rules of use and background assumptions. From Wittgenstein and Heidegger on, modern philosophy has investigated this notion of background meaning, against the earlier idea, pioneered by Augustine, where language is assumed atomistically to be bits of speech that get

fastened arbitrarily onto experience. See, e.g., Charles Taylor, *Philosophical Arguments* (Cambridge: Harvard University Press, 1995), 61-78. Having learned how to use words like "crowd" and "people," I can, for example, give a speech and look out at what I see as a crowd of people. Wittgenstein, however, would ask for the context, or language game, in which "crowd of people" operates. When a security guard in a police state discloses the existence of a "crowd of people" she is likely to be engaging in the language game of warning: warning the troops, that is, to put on combat gear and unleash police dogs. When I say the same words, I am probably congratulating myself on attracting an audience.

28. Barrett, ed., *Lectures*, 59.

29. See, e.g., theological models laid out by Leora Batnitzky (and respondents Robert Gibbs and John Cavadini), "On the Suffering of God's Chosen," in *Christianity in Jewish Terms*, ed. Tikvah Frymer-Kensky, et al. (Boulder: Westview Press, 2000), 203-37. I choose this selection because it so aptly indicates the theological propensity to discuss suffering in the abstract rather than to confront any specific suffering of a single real human being.

30. As reported in *The New York Times*, March 31, 2006.

31. See the remarks by Raymond J. Lawrence, Jr., in "Can Prayers Heal? Critics Say Studies Go Past Science's Reach" (*New York Times* [October 10, 2004], 32). The article contains critiques other than my own of the experiments in question.

32. Roy A. Rappaport, *Ecology, Meaning, and Religion* (Berkeley: North Atlantic Books, 1979), 117, 208, 209, discusses the *Sh'ma* along with other creed-like statements as sacred postulates, unverifiable but also unfalsifiable, and, therefore, endorsable ritually even by people who might otherwise, in rational conversation, question what they actually mean.

33. See Stanley Jeyarajah Tambiah, *Culture, Thought, and Social Action* (Cambridge: Harvard University Press, 1985), 145.

34. See Rappaport, *Ecology*, 179-80.

35. Paul Ames, "85 years after World War I, Flanders Fields Still Yield `Harvest of bones'" (Associated Press Report, November 10, 2003).

36. On photography and suffering, see Susan Sontag, *Regarding the Pain of Others* (New York: Farrar, Straus

and Giroux, 2003). Citations of James and Woolf, 25, 26.

———

Dr. Lawrence A. Hoffman received his rabbinic ordination and Ph.D. from Hebrew Union College, and has served on its New York faculty since 1973. From 1984-1987 he directed its School of Sacred Music, and in 2003 was named Barbara and Stephen Friedman Professor in Liturgy, Worship and Ritual. He is past-president of the North American Academy of Liturgy, and co-founder of "Synagogue 2000," a transdenominational project for synagogue transformation. His twenty-six books include The Canonization of the Synagogue Service *(University of Notre Dame, 1979);* Beyond the Text *(Indiana University, 1987);* Covenant of Blood: Circumcision and Gender in Rabbinic Judaism *(University of Chicago, 1995) and* Rethinking Synagogues: A New Vocabulary for Congregational Life *(Jewish Lights, 2006).*

Mediating the Mediator: A Cultural Theology of Culture

PETE WARD

In *Consuming Religion* Vincent Miller argues that a consumer culture represents a significant challenge for the Christian faith.[1] Consumer culture, he says, commodifies religious symbols and practices. This is corrosive because commodification unhooks practices and symbols from historic traditions and communities of faith (13). As a committed Catholic, Miller is concerned that religious cultures and communities should attempt to resist the negative effects of consumerism. Yet he is also highly critical of theological engagement with consumer culture. Theologians, he says, prefer to discuss consumerism in relation to the history of ideas and anthropology. For Miller this is a mistake. "Whatever the origins of consumer desire in modern metaphysics and anthropology, it is currently sustained not primarily by an incorrigible commitment to pernicious ideas but by a host of economic, social and cultural structures and practices" (115).

Consumer culture, he argues, is not really a culture at all. It is not wedded to any particular worldview or ethos. Rather it is a "set of interpretative habits and dispositions supported by a variety of practices and infrastructures for engaging elements of any culture" (194). The habitual response of theologians to consumerism is to attempt to wrestle the issue onto familiar philosophical grounds. Thus they seek to engage consumerism through questions of cultural content and ontology (4). These strategies miss the mark, says Miller, because they fail to recognise the nature of consumerism and the way it operates both in the church and in the wider society. This does not mean that such concerns are irrelevant, simply that they require methods and ways of seeing that engage more directly with the nature of contemporary culture and society. "There are certainly connections to be made between one's theology of creation or understanding of the incarnation and the practice of daily life, but such correlations are seldom direct applications" (13).

A cultural theology of culture must be particular. This means that it must be situated in the historical and the social. Miller's pessimism concerning the impact of consumerism on contemporary religion is a starting point for such a cultural theology. This essay is a dialogue with the two points raised by Miller: firstly, his largely pessimistic evaluation of the impact of consumer culture on the church, its symbols and practices; secondly, his sense that theologians need to develop new methods of analysis and understanding of the way that contemporary consumer culture operates. A cultural theology therefore must not only focus on particular communicative and social practices in contemporary culture, it also needs to utilise ways of reading and understanding culture. At the same time I believe that theology should be about God. A cultural theology therefore sets out to explore the mediation of God in culture. Such an enterprise sits within a tradition or canon of theological debate and creativity. A cultural theology therefore does not rest with the interpretation of the cultural as mediation, but it sets this within a wider Christian discourse. Engagement with the tradition functions primarily as a creative resource for this cultural theology. Insights from previous periods and cultural situations are used to develop a persuasive, situated, and committed account of the mediation of God in culture.

Theology as Sociology

This treatment of the theological and mediation echoes John Milbank's call for a theology as sociology. The general perception of the argument in *Theology and Social Theory*[2] is that theologians need no longer engage with social science or cultural analysis.[3] I believe this is to misread the direction of his thinking. Milbank's starting point is that theology either positions or is positioned by secular discourses (1). The timidity of theology has meant that it has frequently borrowed a "fundamental account of society and history" and then sought theological insights that "cohere with it" (380). This enterprise is mistaken, argues Milbank, because no such account, which is "neutral, rational and universal," exists (380). In these circumstances, he says, theology must itself act as an account of the social. This involves a fundamental shift in what it means to think theologically. So he argues that "the claim here is not that theology, conceived in broadly traditional fashion, can now add to its competence certain new, 'social' pronouncements. On the contrary the claim is that all theology has to re-conceive itself as a kind of 'Christian Sociology': that is to say as the explication of a socio-linguistic practice, or as the re-narration of this practice as it has historically developed" (381).

Milbank's notion of theology as sociology is highly suggestive. He envisions the expansion of tools of analysis and ways of seeing traditionally linked to theology. Where his perspective is problematic however is the way that "Theology" appears to be disembodied and reified. A cultural theology would not accept the continuation of such assumptions because "Theology" in the way it is used here by Milbank simply doesn't exist. What does exist are theologians, academics, church officials, and preachers who make use of ideas and texts and conventions for their own ends. A cultural theology therefore must be situated and particular. A similar problem with Milbank arises from his location of theology as the dominant discourse. In place of a rather triumphalist air I would locate theological discourse within communities and identities. Here identity and ideas about God are linked by the social. A cultural theology is engaged in by people for certain ends and purposes. It is this commitment that situates social theory in relation to the traditions, canon, and interpreta-

tive conventions and practices of Christians and the churches. It is within this community, and to further these aims and purposes, that the social and the theological are to be negotiated.

Mediation and a Cultural Theology of Culture

Cultural theology accepts that the transcendent is mediated within culture. In his treatment of popular music, Keith Negus says that mediation operates in three ways: first, mediation as intermediary action; second, mediation as transmission; and third, mediation as evident in social relationships.[4] Mediation as intermediary action relates to the activities of individuals and organisations such as record companies, music producers, publicists, and festival organisers. Corresponding to the idea of "production" within the cultural circuit, the action of intermediaries can be read as "producing," but at the same time by engaging in the process of production as affecting what is mediated. Mediation as transmission refers to the role of media in distributing and making available popular music. The internet, the radio, and the compact disk are a means of transmission. In transmission it is recognised that something "passes between" or bridges a gap between parties. Transmission enables, but it also limits the range of expression. Thus there are conventions and limitations to television formats and the popular concert. Finally mediation, says Negus, is situated within social relationships. The consumption and the cultures that characterise the agency of fans mediate popular music and situate it in the social in ways. The activity of groups of people in relation to popular music rearticulates songs with other arenas of meaning-making and significance.

Negus takes his account of mediation from Raymond Williams's *Keywords*.[5] In his account of the usage of mediation Williams draws on early English uses of the term in Chaucer where the mediation of an intermediary refers to a reconciling action between two adversaries. Mediation, says Williams, also carries the sense of the means of transmission or agency. The notion of an intermediary is "repeatedly used of the intercession of Christ between God and man" (171). In addition, through German idealist philosophy, says Williams, mediation also came to carry notions of reconciliation between God and humanity (171). From this it is possible to begin to see a connection between ideas of mediation and the specifically theological. Following Williams's lead it is possible to see how the idea of mediation holds the potential for a dialogue between contemporary understandings of popular culture and rich theological themes. In particular, in the concept of mediation lies not only a Christology, and along with it an implicit doctrine of the Trinity, but also notions of soteriology. When these themes are articulated with the complex reading of mediation offered by Negus a theological/cultural perspective emerges. This synoptic view offers the possibility of a cultural theology of culture.

This cultural theology of culture is developed first through particular accounts of mediation. To "embody" and situate this treatment of culture I have chosen six short case studies where the practices and symbols of the Christian Church are commodified in a consumer culture. I want by this means to extend the discussion with Miller through particular accounts of mediation. Following the case studies I develop a threefold cultural theology. The first section deals with discourse and the Trinity, the second section is soteriological, and the third ecclesiological.

Case One: Iris DeMent. On Lifeline the country singer Iris DeMent delivers stripped-down and passionate renditions of old time gospel songs and hymns. These include Fanny Crosby's "Blessed Assurance" and William Walford's "Sweet Hour of Prayer." DeMent introduces the songs in the sleeve notes of the CD through her own family biography. She describes how when times were tough and life was too much, her mother would sit down at the piano and sing

these songs. The songs seemed to bring resolution and calm to her mother, explains DeMent. Recently she herself has undergone bad times, and in a phone call her mother told her what she should do: "Well Iris! You gotta get to a pe-yan-a!" DeMent explains the significance of this advice: "These songs aren't about religion. At least for me they aren't. They're about something bigger than that. There was an urgency in my mother's voice when she sang that came out of desperation, a great need. When I called her that day and she heard the sinking tone in my voice she did what any compassionate person would do, she threw me a lifeline."[6]

Robert Wuthnow's observation that growing numbers of Americans appear to identify themselves as "spiritual but not religious," and similar insights from Lyon and Roof, can be read as a direct challenge to the survival of the church.[7] Clearly for Iris DeMent these songs have been disconnected from an immediate ecclesial context. At the same time her story offers a tantalising sense that while she may prefer to keep a distance from "religion" the transformational impact of the practice of singing hymns has not died. Indeed it is precisely because these songs offer a "lifeline" that she wishes to share them with the rest of the world. For Miller the commodification of hymns on a country music CD might well be problematic because it bypasses ecclesial life. This seems to me to miss the point. The real question concerns transcendence and transformation. In the singing of these hymns, and in the resolution that such a practice entails, can we assume that the absence of an ecclesial context automatically means the absence of God? Put in more personal terms, when Iris is singing these hymns is God actively present to her and for her? The practice of singing sacred songs in church we might regard with some confidence as an occasion for divine encounter, especially if accompanied by a testimony similar to that given by DeMent. When we meet this affective dimension of faith outside of the church (rather like Peter's encounter with Cornelius in

Acts 10) I suggest we are similarly challenged to expand our horizons.

Case 2: Vivaldi. Country music has a long tradition of Christian songs. When we shift genre to the classical tradition, sacred music has a long and distinguished place in the canon of accepted works. There is something of a revival at present in the performance and recording of liturgical music. The classical music charts are a testament to the continued popularity of ecclesiastical music. I estimate that at least half of the CDs on sale in my own local music store in Oxford are in the genre of church music. An edition of Vivaldi's vespers is a fine example of these developments.[8] Recorded in 2003, the musical score has been reconstructed from a number of different fragments of previously lost manuscripts. The reconstruction is designed to present the liturgy as it would have been conducted by Vivaldi in Venice at the convent church of San Lorenzo (sleeve notes, 21).

What is interesting is how the record company represents what is clearly sacred music. Most sacred music is represented through the use of ecclesiastical imagery: stained glass windows, a pietà or similar statue, or perhaps a renaissance painting of a crucifixion or another religious scene. In contrast, the Italian company Naïve have packaged Vivaldi's work with a striking image of a young girl. She is clothed in white with a garland of white roses around her blond hair. Her eyes are closed, yet she appears to be looking down as if in a moment of reflection. Her slightly parted lips are colored pink, and they are set in relief by her pale complexion. The impression is something of a cross between one of Zeffereli's film stars and a young Gwyneth Paltrow.

The image is sexy and contemporary, but it articulates with the sensuous nature of Vivaldi's score and the performance of the Concerto Italiano and the featured soloists. It locates the religious and the mystical in a new frame. Again

here is an example of what Miller may see as the commodification of the Catholic tradition. The question here is similar to that at play in DeMent's account of the significance of religious music in daily life. The music as text, and the encoded nature of its representation, give no clue as to the significance of this music for those of us who consume it. The question is the same: "Is God absent or present to us when we listen to this music? If God is present what are the theological implications of such agency?" Clearly the intention is to dislocate this music from its ecclesiastical context, but does its re-articulation locate it in another space? Alessandrini argues that even in seventeenth- and eighteenth-century Italy the ecclesiastical context of music such as Vivaldi's was so elided with the aesthetic as to be ambiguous in its theological significance (sleeve notes, 26). If this is the case within an ecclesiastical context, could not the opposite be also the case when this music is consumed outside of the church and apart from its liturgy?

Case 3: Vineyard music. The first in a series of recordings featuring worship leaders from the UK and Ireland, *Hungry* represents the extent to which the charismatic church has embraced a commercial culture.[9] I first encountered this CD while on a trip to South Africa. Vineyard had just released the recording through its South African distribution company. My hosts in Johannesburg told me that this was "the latest thing," and—despite being from the Baptist Church—wherever I went the music from the Vineyard was being used in their meetings. The songs, which were written and developed in congregations in Dublin and London and other parts of Britain, were travelling to another continent and a new context and situation. This is of course the intention of the Vineyard Church; they have their own linked company, Vineyard Music, whose aim is to package and distribute the "products" that arise from the distinctive culture of their local church congregations.

Inspired by this recording I started to use one of the songs, "Be the Centre," in my own local church where I was occasionally invited to lead worship. The song has a Celtic feel, and comes from the Vineyard Church in Dublin. It speaks of Jesus being the fire in our hearts and the wind in our sails. This song meant a great deal to me and to those of us in our local church. We were one of the new initiatives in the Anglican Church, and our focus was the desire to be a church for young people. For the five or six of us gathered in the cold empty church this vision of a church open and welcoming to young people seemed a long way off. "Be the Centre" offered a focus and vision in worship for our hopes and endeavours.

I give this personal illustration because I want to convey a sense that our ecclesial context had its own authenticity. In this rather gritty and testing context the commodification of religious culture enabled our worship. This was only possible because of the way that the song had been recorded and sold. So, against Miller, I would argue that for the charismatic tradition the commercial development of record companies and the commodification of worship music is the tradition, or at least it is the means by which the tradition circulates and reproduces itself.

Case 4: Taizé. In a tiny French village in Burgundy close to Cluny, Brother Roger founded his ecumenical community.[10] Its origins lay in a concern for reconciliation and ecumenical relationships following the Second World War. Every summer thousands of young people travel to this remote part of France to join the community of brothers, who now number around a hundred, as they sing their songs, spend time in silence, and share their vision for the church and the world.

With its ecumenical perspectives and concern for reconciliation the Taizé community has always charted a precarious course between and among ecclesial traditions.[11] The liturgy combines symbolism and practices from the Catholic, Protestant, and Orthodox traditions. The more recent addition of Orthodox-style domes to the Church of the Reconciliation at Taizé is a conscious borrowing of tradition, as is the display of icons inside the church. From this "bricolage" something distinctive and new has arisen. Taizé has produced a distinctive religious culture.

The way that this culture is distributed is through products, in particular through the songs that Taizé uses in worship. In the community's shop CDs, DVDs, music-only recordings, and various music books are on sale. Through the use of the songs individuals are able to transport something of Taizé back to their home communities and churches. Taizé is a male-only monastic community; it has not established a lay community, as exists for instance among the Franciscans. As a result, while young people visit them there is no easy way for them to "join" Taizé. Of course women cannot be a part of the community at all. Taizé is not a church or a substitute for church. Its ecumenical vision is about reconciliation and renewal from within. Thus it operates as a movement or a network sustained by pilgrimage, through the songs and liturgy generated by the community, and increasingly through the use of the Internet. Taizé has had an enormous impact on the Catholic Church and I am sure that Miller would feel at home there. This familiarity might mean that the commodification and consumer-based nature of the culture of Taizé might be somewhat disguised. Taizé feels like church, but on closer inspection it is every church and no church. In trying to be ecumenical it has become postmodern.

Case 5: WWJD bracelets. The WWJD bracelet represents a unique event in what Colleen McDannell calls "material Christianity."[12] The WWJD phenomenon was probably the first teen craze within the Christian Church, with millions of these bracelets and other fashion items being sold in the US and the UK. WWJD stands for "What Would Jesus Do?" For Miller, I suspect WWJD would represent the worst of commercialised religion and commodification. Again I would like to take issue with this reading.

For the younger teenager identity is closely linked to style and image. Fashion is therefore more than simply clothes. A sense of self and a sense of belonging are constructed using "things." We might identify this creative activity of young people as necessary work. It is necessary because it is linked to selfhood and community. The commodities of consumerism are therefore the stuff out of which identities are shaped—or rather the meanings that are associated with them are the stuff from which identities are shaped.

WWJD is significant because the Christian faith is largely absent from the material world of the younger teenager. Churches do not speak the language or share in the discourse of style, image, and fashion. An exception to this might be the cross when it is worn as an earring or a necklace, but the cross as a symbol has become somewhat ubiquitous, and this may be a point in support of Miller's thesis, because the cross has been devalued by its use. It may be an urban myth, but a young woman was overheard in a jewellers asking for a silver cross on a chain. When she was asked which one she said she wanted the one with the little man on it. WWJD bracelets, however, sit alongside the white "Make Poverty History" and the BBC sponsored blue anti-bullying wristbands as a potent signifier in the world of the younger teenager.

Case 6: The Cretan labyrinth. The labyrinth has a long and much mythologized place in the history of religions. The Cretan labyrinth in particular is rich in pre-Christian and Christian symbolism. Interest in labyrinths has grown apace in the last few years. In particular, evangelical Christians have appropriated the symbol and the practices of making and walking laby-

rinths as part of a wider move towards spiritual practices. Alternative worship groups in the UK, in particular a gathering of young Christians in London linked to Vaux and Grace congregations, have reframed the labyrinth combining a series of prayer stations with their own labyrinth design. Those walking the labyrinth are guided along their journey by wearing headphones with a CD that has prayers and music to help with meditation. This innovative creation was picked up by the organisation Youth for Christ, and a tour was organised around the main cathedrals and churches in the UK. In the US the publishing company Group have marketed this version of the labyrinth giving it the name "Prayer Walk."

The contemporary Christian use of the labyrinth is an example of the way that symbols and practices circulate in religious traditions. Miller of course may be critical of the way that this symbol is dislocated from an original context by these processes. The marketing of the "Prayer Walk" in the US is obviously a commodification of this ancient symbol. Yet here again the productive processes associated with a publishing company's selling this item should perhaps be seen as the means whereby this symbol becomes re-embedded in a new ecclesial context. The combination of an organisation such as Youth for Christ taking the labyrinth to places such as Canterbury Cathedral and York Minister is potent in symbolism. Having groups of young people, and even the curious tourist, walking the labyrinth in these places suggests a new articulation of this symbol. What is happening in the spiritual journey of individuals is not accessible without a more in-depth analysis of this practice, yet it still poses the question: is God absent or present within this new cultural formation? If God is present how is this to be understood theologically?

The case studies as a starting point for theological creativity. These six case studies are a brief snapshot of the way that contemporary cultural change and communication are being utilised within and beyond the Christian community. Through consumer culture symbols and practices are circulated and carry meaning. A cultural theology needs to be able to travel beyond the "thing" to the significance invested in the symbol. For example, in the representation of the Vivaldi vespers we see the way that the record company has tried to reframe music that had its origin in the liturgical life of the Catholic Church in a contemporary frame of reference. The meaning of this recording, however, does not rest with the encoding of the marketing department of Naïve records or the imagery of the cover. The music itself and its text afford a diverse range of interpretation. To travel into the significance of this recording we need to gain an insight into the affective dimensions of this music. Representation cannot simply be reduced to a theory based on the manipulation of consumers by commercial companies. The integrity of the text, and the score and its performance on the recording, indicate that meaning is open for those of us who listen to the music. Meaning needs to be sought in the articulations made by the audience. The sonic space of the recording affords a connectivity to a Christian text and sensibility.

Similar observations pertain to the adoption of the labyrinth by evangelical Christians in the UK and the US. The meaning of this symbol cannot be read from its previous historical contexts. Its re-articulation means that its representation shifts with cultural reference points. This is a new discursive context. The symbol operates within a network of other symbols. The effect of this is to create a new context for meaning linked to the symbol. The link between the evangelical youth organisation Youth for Christ and the ecclesial context of a cathedral creates a new discursive formation within which individuals may locate a specific practice of prayer and meditation. The way that the commodification of this symbol and practice

operates indicates that through discourse a new tradition emerges. A person once said to me that in a rural congregation tradition was fluid. If you tried something new and people liked it then it became traditional and they expected it to happen again. If they didn't like it, it was regarded as an unwelcome innovation and generally resisted. Tradition understood as discourse is not static; it is in a constant flux. Representation is the way that symbols and practices are dislocated and relocated within structures of meaning.

Increasingly information and communication technologies are shaping how meanings are circulated within the Christian community. For charismatic churches such as Vineyard these processes have been enthusiastically adopted as part of their ecclesial life. Yet charismatics are not alone in their use of the media to generate a religious culture. The influence of the Taizé Community extends way beyond rural France through its music and its promotion as a place of pilgrimage. Record companies and worship leaders, religious communities and pilgrimage, combine in the production of religious culture. Yet discourse is articulated through the agency of consumers. The meaning of Vineyard or Taizé does not lie solely in the texts of the music, or in the institutions that they generate and from which these texts emerge. The meaning of Taizé also lies in the identifications made by thousands of young people, and those of us who are not so young, who are making sense of ourselves and encounter God as we sing the songs. Similarly with Vineyard, we cannot interpret the songs through their lyrics alone, or even through the strengths and problems of the charismatic communities from which they emerge. The songs are carried within discourse and are relocated through the identification made by individuals and communities around the world.

For critics such as Miller these accommodations with consumer culture may be less problematic because of their ecclesial context. The case of Iris DeMent's recording *Lifeline* may be more problematic. Yet here also I would argue that the songs and the way that they are performed contain their own integrity. They operate affectively outside of their ecclesial context in much the same way as they do within the church. Of course the dislocation of divine encounter from specific ecclesial relationships means that something different is taking place. The question this prompts relates to the activity of the Spirit in individuals as they listen. The case studies focus the attention on the complexity of mediation. Within this complexity the starting point for a cultural theology of culture relates to the presence or absence of God. This question emerges not simply in relation to meanings which might be inscribed by productive processes, for instance the ecclesial context from which the Vineyard songs have come. Neither can the question be answered entirely in relation to their textual richness and content. So the recording of Vivaldi's vespers as liturgical text does not in itself suggest an answer to the question. Nor can it be read solely from the social relationships and practices within which symbols and practices are consumed. Singing worship songs and walking labyrinths do not in themselves constitute an encounter with God. The question of the presence or the absence of God relates to the complexity of mediation in all of these ways. This means that the theological question of mediation needs to be addressed in a multi-layered way.

Bureaucracy and Epiphany

The presence and absence of God in mediation can be addressed in a variety of ways. The omnipresence of God might suggest that God is always and everywhere near. An appreciation of the world and human making as aspects of creation sustained within and around by the Spirit of creation might also be a fruitful source of a theology of culture. Similarly notions of the *imago Dei* afford an understanding of human expression as akin to the life of God. Fruitful as these avenues of thought may be, they introduce a mechanistic or inevitable or natural dimension into a theology of culture. They develop a bureaucratic reflex that can downplay the relational, the intimate, and the particular. As such they represent background lighting rather than the ray of sunlight, the hum of the bass amp as opposed to the punchy riff. The bureaucratic has its place but it does not set the world alight. Epiphany however speaks of the revealing moments, the places where God is powerfully present, mediated in culture rather than naturally or automatically there. This is mediation where through revealing intimacy is achieved. It is mediation that reconciles. The case studies focus attention on the way that consumer culture operates as mediation. The theological challenge of these particular texts and social practices rests in the possibility that God might be revealed and present. Mediation mediating the mediator.

In many ways this is the same question addressed in Karl Barth's opening volume of the *Church Dogmatics*. For Barth the church has a commission to engage in talk about God. Preaching and the sacraments are distinctive as proclamation because of this commission. The distinctiveness of proclamation comes from the Word of God.[13] Preaching is not necessarily proclamation. It must "ever and again" become so. It is this becoming which makes the church the church (88). Proclamation is not distinctive because of a particular message or set of values. God's Word is the content of proclamation and as such it becomes an object for human study, but as proclamation it can never be objectified. In proclamation it "presents and places itself as an object over and against us" (91). "We have it as it gives itself to us" (92). This is an event of revelation. A revealing—or, as I prefer it in the context of the present discussion, an "epiphany." In this encounter the humanity of those who proclaim, says Barth, is not cast aside because proclamation becomes itself an event among other human events and can be read on this level. As Christ became a true man and his humanity continues throughout eternity, proclamation exists as a human acting and making. Yet there is a new "robe of righteousness thrown over it" and its earthly character takes on another kind of event. Real proclamation is an event where human talk about God becomes a place where God speaks about himself (95). Talk about God rests on the canon of Scripture, but Scripture, like the proclamation of the church, is itself a human recollection of revelation (102). The Bible is the means by which the church remembers past revelation and is "called to an expectation of His future revelation and is thus summoned and guided to proclamation and empowered for it" (111). As such the Bible is not God's past revelation. Both proclamation and Scripture are conditioned by the Word of God revealed. God with us (116).

Revelation as a revealing is conditioned by the act of revelation. What this means, says Barth, is that "revelation in fact does not differ from the person of Jesus Christ nor from the revelation accomplished in him" (119). By talking of revelation we inevitably speak therefore of the God who was made flesh and dwelt among us. This takes us to the Trinity. The Word made flesh is the will of the Father and the sending of the Son and the Spirit. It is the knowledge of God from God and of "light in light" (119). It is God who reveals Godself (296). God's speaking is not to be distinguished from God. Revelation is a personal address that confronts humanity. The Word of God is always "mediated" and so if the Word of God is God's self then Scripture and the preaching of the church are not to be taken as self-evidently and inevitably revelation. Rather they become so as an event, as a free act of God's grace. "It is in this freedom and through grace that God reveals himself as the Lord" (306).

Barth's treatment of revelation connects mediation with a Christologically articulated Trinitarian theology. The preaching of the church is acknowledged as mediation. It is human speech, and in our sense cultural. At the same time it is the place where God reveals himself. God's revelation is an event and act received in faith. Revelation is not inevitable; it is not negotiated or deduced from a specific content of what has been revealed in Scripture or in past proclamation. Revelation is dynamic and personal; as such it is focused in Jesus Christ and in the reconciliation he brings. Mediation mediates the mediator. The case studies suggest that mediation can be a place of revelation. Here attention focuses on the freedom of God to be present as event. The case studies suggest that at a particular place God may be present. What Barth brings to this is the sense that such "epiphanies" are located in God's self. Revelation is Trinitarian and its content is Jesus Christ. God's freedom to be present is a Trinitarian event. The freedom of the Spirit is an epiphany and event.

Discourse and the Trinity

The case studies show how ecclesial life is being extended through consumer culture. An example of this is seen in the way that Vineyard Churches use their record company as a way of circulating not just music but a particular expression of charismatic worship. This embodied intimacy manifested at a local level is transmitted through mediation from community to community and from continent to continent. Technology and commodification enable these relations within which individuals and groups participate in the life of God. Communion is mediated in commodification.

From a quite different ecclesial position John Zizioulas develops his discussion of the church and of God through categories of ontology, but he locates this ontology in ideas of relationship and community. Thus for Zizioulas ecclesial identity, or ecclesial being, indicates an ultimate reality that rests on God mediated in communion.[14] So he can argue that "the mystery of the Church, even in its institutional dimension, is deeply bound to the very being of man, to the being of the world and to the very being of God."[15] As a member of the church the believer is in the "image of God," says Zizioulas (15). It was this ecclesial experience of communion that generated and directed the thinking of the Fathers. Ecclesial identity and communion were of particular significance for Athanasius and Irenaeus in their consideration of the being of God. "This experience revealed something very important: the being of God could be known only through personal relationships and personal love. Being means life and life means communion" (16). So, argues Zizioulas, the ontology of the Fathers emerges out of the eucharistic life of the church. Communion and being are therefore dynamically and relationally connected. Thus he asserts that "God has no ontological content, no true being, apart from communion" (17).

Communion therefore makes things be. Without communion nothing exists, including God. In communion, in the Eucharist, the church contemplates the life of the Holy Trinity as communion. In such contemplation lay the realization of humanity's true being as an "image of Gods own being" (21). Thus the Eucharist is not the practice of a church that already exists; rather it is the Eucharist that constitutes the church's being (21). Participation in communion is participation in the very life of God. "The life of the Eucharist is the life of God himself … It is the life of communion with God, such as exists within the Trinity and is actualised within the members of the Eucharistic community" (81). Thus, says Zizioulas, "Knowledge and communion are identical" (81). This, says Alan Torrance, is the strength of Zizioulas's position. "Divine communication in the context of faith is an event of communion and demands to be conceived, therefore, in terms of participation within communion (and hence the 'mutuality') of the triune life."[16]

Zizioulas is not alone among contemporary theologians in making the link between ecclesial identity, the being of the church, and the being of God. Whilst he expresses reservations about Zizioulas's understanding of communion in the church, Miroslav Volf does approve of what he calls "a social understanding of salvation." He identifies this version of "social salvation" as being held in common within the Catholic and the Orthodox traditions of the church as exemplified by Zizioulas and Karl Rahner respectively.[17] David Cunningham is also in general agreement with these judgments. He observes that despite differences over the meaning and the use of terminology the link between relationality and the being of God advocated by Zizioulas is widely shared in contemporary Trinitarian theology.[18]

A relational understanding of the Trinity is widespread. At the same time these views have often been utilised by theologians to combat perceived notions of individualism in modernity. Volf's assessment that in modernity the ecclesiological community is being eaten away by the "worm of modernity" is a common theological position.[19] Zizioulas's assertion that modernity has eroded a theological conception of the person should also be set in this context (27). This resistant position, which seems to be characteristic of contemporary theological interpretations of culture, may be going somewhat against the direction of the deeper flow of communitarian and communicative notions of the Trinity

In his discussion of mission and participation Paul Fiddes utilises the notion of "representation."[20] Representation, he says, lies at the heart of Zizioulas's work. It is in the Eucharist that the believer encounters and is taken up into the holy life of the divine. Communion and communication are integral to a relational and participative Trinitarian theology. Torrance also makes this kind of link between communion and communication. He argues that in the debate on analogy Zizioulas's theology of participation, his "analysis of capacity and incapacity, and his relating of communion and communication, personhood and truthfulness," are profoundly significant (*Persons*, 305). If, like Fiddes and Torrance, we want to make use of Zizioulas's theology, then we are forced to move from ontology to a more operational theology.

Thus notions of relationship in communication and representation are present as culture. Liturgy should therefore properly be understood as participation in God and also as practice and discourse. At the same time ecclesial relationships are both representational and discursive, and they are also mediations of divine life.

Contemplation and Cultural Capital

Communion is mediated through the practices of representation and identification. A cultural theology of culture recognises that in mediation practices of faith operate in discourse. At the heart of a Trinitarian reading of the cultural life of God lies an interaction between epiphany and attention. What is at stake in the case studies is the extent to which the practices of mediation create an occasion for contemplation. Contemplation must not be routinised or bureaucratised into a general possibility; rather it should be located in the particularity of epiphany.

For Athanasius the image of God in humanity rests not only on the creative imprint of the Logos, but humanity through the creative work of the Word shares with the Word the same reason that shaped the world.[21] The image of God is not seen by Athanasius as a "natural" or inherent gift. The divine imprint must be maintained and sustained through a continual attention and contemplation of the Word. "By nature, of course, man is mortal, since he was made from nothing; but he bears also the Likeness of Him Who is, and if he preserves that Likeness through constant contemplation, then his nature is deprived of its power and he remains incorrupt" (30).

With corruption this constant contemplation was interrupted and humanity became "bereft of grace" (33). For Athanasius mortality is reinforced through a turning of attention from the things that are eternal to those that are corruptible. The shift of attention towards the corruptible leads in turn to corruption, and the effects of mortality are unchecked by grace (33).

It is for the restoration and rescue of humanity that the Word "entered the world." The Word had of course not been far from the world, for, says Athanasius, "no part of creation had ever been without Him Who, while ever abiding in union with the Father, yet fills all things that are" (33). Now however the Word enters the world in a new way, "stooping to our level in His love and Self-revealing to us" (33). The recreation of the image of God in humanity required that death and corruption be addressed. Redemption operates firstly as a renewal of mortality through the Word which takes our flesh upon himself. Like a king entering a city his glory transforms it from within (35ff). Secondly, through his death and resurrection death and corruption are "utterly abolished" (49). The restoration of the image enables a renewal of attention and contemplation. This contemplation is itself aided by the incarnation of the Word. The Saviour of the world, seeing that people were focused on "sensible things," became himself an object for the senses (44).

"There were thus two things which the Saviour did for us by becoming Man. He banished death from us and made us anew; and, invisible and imperceptible as in Himself He is, He became visible through His works and revealed Himself as the Word of the Father, the Ruler and King of the whole creation" (44-45).

Recreation through the restoration of humanity in the Word of God is linked to the sustaining dynamic of contemplation. The visibility of the Word enables the dynamic to recommence in the renewed creature. Restoration and contemplation lead to participation in the divine. The incarnation operates at a number of levels to bring unity between humanity and divinity. "For He was made man that we might be made God; and He manifested Himself by a body that we might receive the idea of the unseen Father; and He endured the insolence of men that we might inherit immortality."[22]

Mediation relocates the practice of attention and contemplation. Through its operations

the symbols and practices of the church are
transmitted beyond understood ecclesial frameworks. The fluid nature of practice stretches
ecclesial life. Contemplation however has its
proper object. Mediation by definition relates
to sensible things. This does not mean, however,
that attention to mediated practices and symbols
will of necessity turn towards the corrupting
and the corruptible. In the incarnation the Word
enters the world of the senses. It is in mediation
that the Word is mediated. In mediation the
Word becomes the object of contemplation. An
example of this can be seen in how the case studies illustrate the way that songs and hymns may
mediate Christ. Such a proposal seems appropriate. The content of the songs clearly afford the
interpretation that they might mediate Christ.
There is a correspondence between text and the
one who may be revealed.

With the labyrinth this correspondence
clearly becomes more problematic. The Cretan
labyrinth is a pre-Christian symbol. Among contemporary Christian groups labyrinths such as
this are being re-appropriated as part of a widespread turn to practices and rituals. Unlike the
case study of the hymns, the labyrinth, as symbol
and text, cannot be read as corresponding to
Christian revelation. This does not however preclude the possibility that in its use it might not
provide the occasion for epiphany. The labyrinth
is mediated through the social relations and
practices of those who use it. In other words, it
is mediated by the pre-knowledge or theological capital that are brought to it. Theological
capital, to adapt Bourdieu, acknowledges that
those Christians and non-Christians who walk
the labyrinth bring to the practice particular
understandings and ways of being. Theological
capital allows individuals to re-position rather
than be positioned by what might be transmitted
through mediation.

Capital and the mediation of social
relationships suggest that texts must be read in
relation to their use. Texts may afford, or indeed
not fund, particular readings. Yet the mediation of texts must be located in particular ways
of using and understanding. A good example
of this might be the assumption that many
contemporary charismatic songs are based on
repetition and void of theological content. Such
a conclusion might be justified based solely on
the lyrics of some of the songs. The notion of
capital, however, means that the practices related
to charismatic worship must be read through
the pre-knowledge brought by individuals to the
song. Theological capital might, for instance,
locate the ambiguous and anonymous "you" of
charismatic worship in a coherent framework.
Just as with the labyrinth so also with charismatic worship, attention and contemplation must be
linked to the ways that individuals and groups
embody and indwell practices and symbols.

Identification, Transformation, and Habitus

Identification refers to the way that individuals
construct identity in relation to representation and discourse. These identifications are
internalised in structuring structures that can
be observed as people engage in sacred practice.
Attention and contemplation are a participation in the life of God mediated in discourse.
Participation is not just affective. Epiphany leads
to intimacy and intimacy to transformation.

In Paul's second letter to the Corinthians
transformation is linked to the work of the Holy
Spirit. Paul's assertions concerning the freedom
of the Spirit form part of a wider struggle over
authority and leadership. At its heart this is a
struggle for the content and meaning of the
Gospel, and it turns on the work of the Holy
Spirit. The Spirit, says Gordon Fee, is "presup-
positional" to the faith of the early church. As
is often the case with what is presupposed, he
says, these areas often remain theologically
unexamined.[23] This means that in Paul's writing
this experience of the Spirit often underlies or is
utilised in the context of quite separate debates.
Yet it remains true that "in the case of the Spirit
we are dealing with the essential matter of early

Christian experience. Here was how the early church came to appropriate the salvation that Christ had brought" (2). Douglas Cambell also identifies pneumatology as the effective heart of Pauline theology. The work of the Spirit, he says, is linked to "a radical ontological transformation of the person; something only a creator can effect (anticipating this for creation as a whole)."[24] Second Corinthians 3:17-18 and 4:5-6 should be located within this wider social and theological matrix. "Now the Lord is the Spirit, and where the Spirit of the Lord is, there is freedom. And all of us, with unveiled faces, seeing the glory of the Lord as though reflected in a mirror, are being transformed into the same image from one degree of glory to another; for this comes from the Lord, the Spirit" (2 Cor 3:17-18).

This verse brings together a complex discussion from the preceding section of the letter concerning the relationship between Old Covenant and Gospel. Paul's argument relates to the glory of God reflected in Moses' shining face and the fear of the Jews who insisted that Moses should cover his face with a veil. The ministry of the Spirit, says Paul, is also characterised by glory, but this is the glory of the Lord, and believers may gaze upon this glory "unveiled." Sinai was a scene of glory, but this is surpassed by the Spirit; there is no comparison between the two occasions.[25] This is the glory of the Lord, and the glory of the Lord is also the glory of the Gospel. "For it is the God who said, 'Let light shine out of darkness,' who has shone in our hearts to give the light of the knowledge of the glory of God in the face of Jesus Christ" (2 Cor 4:6).

Glory denotes the presence of God. For Jacob Jervell the divine *doxa* is the way God exists and acts. The *doxa* of Christ therefore refers to the presence of God in Christ.[26] Thus the glory of the Lord speaks of the presence of God in Christ and through the work of the Spirit in the believer. Knowledge of God comes from a shining glory seen in the face of Christ, and Christ is the *ikon* of God (2 Cor 4:4). This is the freedom brought by the Spirit, for the believer may see

with an unveiled face. The Spirit is the presence of God and the transforming power of God.[27] Paul's soteriology therefore is made effectual through the work of the Holy Spirit, but it also patterns a Trinitarian economy.

In Second Corinthians 3:8 we see a culturally expressed theology. It would be possible to describe the debates between Paul and the Corinthian church solely in terms of power and social relationships, but this would be somewhat reductive. Talk of glory and the Spirit, of the Lord who is the Image of God, and the Gospel that shines in the light of Christ, could be seen solely as rhetoric or the symbolic exchange of the community, and yet this would appear to impose an interpretation that goes against the grain of the text. At the same time clearly these ideas are embedded in the practices and experience of the early Christians. The power of Paul's rhetoric lies in the appeal to a theological capital. This "knowing" is generated by the working of the Spirit and in practices of faith in which the glory of the Gospel is seen in the shining face of Christ. This is an embodied faith, which has a resonance in the Christian community through its traditions and liturgical practices. This is seen in the way that commentators, whilst locating the ideas in different theological micro-climates and pursuing different projects, have identified with the energy of this Pauline Trinitarian theology of glory. Thus Saint John Chrysostom can speak of the cleansing of the Spirit in baptism as the light of the glory of God, and the believer as like silver reflecting the sun. "For as soon as we are baptized, the soul beameth even more than the sun, being cleansed by the Spirit; and not only do we behold the glory of God, but from it also receive a sort of splendor."[28]

John Calvin's commentary on this passage also reveals a resonance of this imagery for his own understanding of the faith. He writes that "the purpose of the gospel is the restoration in us of the image of God which had been cancelled by sin," and that "this restoration is progressive and goes on during our whole life, because God makes his glory shine in us little by little."[29]

Karl Barth makes a similar use of Second Corinthians 3:18. "And therefore we ourselves are a mirror in whom the Lord sees himself and in whom he discovers his own image, so that confronting us, he takes and uses us as a mirror and we are actually changed into his image. His glory becomes our glory and his image our image."[30]

Writing in the 1960s Philip Hughes speaks in very similar terms of this passage. He says that "to contemplate Him who is the Father's image is progressively to be transformed into that image. The effect of continuous beholding is that we are continuously being transformed into the 'same image,' that is into the likeness of Christ."[31]

What is interesting about these passages from Chrysostom, Calvin, Barth, and Hughes is the use of "we." There is an identification here with the experience of Paul and the community to whom he speaks. The work of the Spirit is part of an enduring identification. Of course this is a cultural identity, and as such cannot be abstracted from the social and relational. Yet the function of these ideas is to animate spiritual longing and ecclesial practice. Fee talks of his study of Pauline pneumatology, and an identification of his own "urgencies" with the urgencies of Saint Paul (*Empowering*, 5). Michael Ramsey forges links between a theology of glory and the liturgical practice of the church. He argues that this notion of glory is integral to the structure of the Christian faith.[32] For Ramsey, and for the other commentators, this structuring is located in the practices of worship common within the Christian church. In other words, a theology of glory is located in places where the veil may be lifted, where the Spirit is active, where glory is made manifest, where the Gospel shines, and where the face of Christ is seen.

In mediation, to speak of the Spirit is to express the freedom of God to be present as Lord. In representation, the light of the Gospel shines in the face of Christ. Mediation however is transformative. It structures the *habitus* of the believer who is transformed by glory. The pres-ence of God is imprinted through contemplation and attention. Epiphany leads to intimacy and participation to transformation.

Liquid Church

Communion with God, as Zizioulas says, is not a practice of the church; rather it is communion that constitutes the church (*Being*, 81). Mediation extends this encounter and as it does so it liquefies ecclesial life. Zizioulas imagines communion and the Eucharist in fairly defined and predetermined ecclesial ways. Barth similarly locates proclamation within the four walls of the local church. The case studies indicate the extent that ecclesial meeting, relationship, and expression are shifting in a mediated consumer culture. The circulation of representation in mediated discourses lifts encounter from the fixed context of the church service.

The church finds itself in this new context somewhere between Pandora and Saint Peter — Pandora in that much of the innovation comes from the activities of Christian communities themselves. A community like Taizé is committed to the existing life, traditions, and institutions of the churches. Vineyard is a movement that is strongly committed to growing local congregations. Yet both of these indicate the extent to which belonging and identity are extended and made more fluid through representation and discourse. Cultural expression and the circulation of products allows a belonging and sense of self that are more fluid and diverse than the local expression. We may try and close the box by insisting on communion and revelation as preaching and the Eucharist performed within an understood ecclesial setting. The challenge of mediation relates to the freedom of the Lord who is the Spirit. Like Saint Peter, the Christian community faces a challenge to think beyond its own assumptions. The life of God, epiphany, intimacy, and transformation, are mediated beyond the walls, and indeed the social relations, of the congregation. This is the Liquid Church.[33]

Liquid Church is characterised by an embracing of mediation. Through representation and discourse new ecclesial identities and relations are brought into being. These relationships can be described as networks of communication. What distinguishes these networks is that they are fluid. Connections are established through the circulation of symbols and practices as mediation. What this means is that connectivity is based on the flow of discourse. In traditional patterns of church, discourse circulates within existing social patterns. In the network established by the fluid mediation, connectivity follows the circulation of representation. Similarly, identities are relocated in mediation. In traditional patterns of church, belonging structures not just the discursive flow, but it also precedes identification with aspects of representation. Mediation reverses this order. Here identification follows the flow of representation. In terms of the case studies, this is illustrated by the place of worship songs in the charismatic movement. In the early days of the renewal movement, charismatics sang worship songs as a part of belonging to the wider renewal movement. For the generation raised on the music of the Vineyard Churches and Soul Survivor, belonging has been restructured and made more fluid. Now the worship songs themselves establish belonging. You belong if you sing the songs rather than the other way round. The songs in themselves however do not constitute identity. It is epiphany, intimacy, and transformation in the glorious freedom of the Spirit mediated by the songs that constitute belonging.

The significance of mediation in contemporary culture is that the church — like Peter in Acts 10 — is faced with the dilemma of having to adjust to the fluid movement of the life of God. For just as the Spirit moved in advance of Peter's framework of reference, and rested upon the gentile Cornelius and his household, the circulation of Christian practices and symbols in the representation and discourses of contemporary culture mediates encounter with God outside of the accepted frameworks of the church. In discourse the symbols and practices of faith are in play, and through the freedom of the Spirit the life of God may also be mediated.

While some may welcome this fluid context and accept that the Spirit is active outside of particular ecclesial boundaries, there is also some hesitancy to embrace these developments. It is accepted that people may encounter God in prayer and spiritual practices outside of the church, but how can faith grow and develop beyond the relational context of the Christian community? This is a significant critique of the idea of a Liquid Church. The challenge here relates not so much to the individuals and groups who encounter God in mediated culture, but it rests with those charged with the ministry of the church itself. Like Peter, the Spirit has moved beyond their frame of reference, and they must in turn face the challenge and find ways to catch up. The current interest in contemporary ecclesiology expressed as Emerging Church in the US and Fresh Expressions of Church in the UK indicates that all is not lost in this respect.

However I feel that the focus on new forms of ecclesial life needs to be informed by the changes that are already taking place in churches. The case studies show how through mediation ecclesial life becomes more fluid, and through representation and mediation new forms of belonging and identity are already being formed. Through mediation symbols and practices are lifted from one context and relocated in another. Mediated through social relations, they suggest the fluidity of tradition. At the same time meaning is constructed through the exercise of theological capital. Capital is built up within social relations. Transmission of theological capital therefore depends on developing sites where individuals and groups may accrue capital and develop *habitus*. The challenge for the Liquid Church is how to allow the freedom of the Spirit to enable individuals to move from epiphany to intimacy and then to transformation. That Christ the mediator is mediated is cause for celebration rather than condemnation, but the spread of mediated symbols and practices in a consumer culture is no excuse for complacency. The Liquid Church must find ways to develop appropriate networks through which the mediated freedom of the Spirit may flow.

ENDNOTES

1. Vincent J. Miller, *Consuming Religion* (London: Continuum, 2004), 72.

2. John Milbank, *Theology and Social Theory: Beyond Secular Reason* (Oxford: Blackwell, 1990).

3. For an example of this see Mark Cartledge, *Practical Theology: Charismatic and Empirical Perspectives* (Carlisle: Paternoster, 2003), 1, n 32.

4. Keith Negus, *Popular Music in Theory: An Introduction* (Cambridge: Polity, 1996), 67-69.

5. Raymond Williams, *Keywords: A Vocabulary of Culture and Society* (Glasgow: Fontana, 1976).

6. Iris DeMent, *Lifeline* (FlariElla Records, 2004), sleeve notes.

7. Robert Wuthnow, *After Heaven: Spirituality in America since the 1950s* (Berkeley: University of California Press, 1998), 2; see also David Lyon, *Jesus in Disneyland: Religion in Postmodern Times* (Malden, Mass.: Polity Press, 2000), ix; Wade Clark Roof, *Spiritual Marketplace: Baby Boomers and the Remaking of American Religion* (Princeton: Princeton University Press, 1999), 33-35.

8. Antonio Vivaldi, *Vespri per l'Assunzione di Maria Vergine.* Concerto Italiano, Rinaldi Alessandrini (Naïve Op 30383).

9. Vineyard Music, *Hungry - Live from London* (Vineyard Music BIC 02).

10. For an account of the origins of the Taizé community see J. L. G. Balado, *The Story of Taizé* (Oxford; Mowbray's, 1980).

11. Balado, *Taizé*, 40 ff.

12. Colleen McDannell, *Material Christianity: Religion and Popular Culture in America* (New Haven: Yale University Press, 1995).

13. Karl Barth, *Church Dogmatics* 1/1 (Edinburgh: T and T Clark, 1975), 47.

14. See Roger E. Olson and Christopher A. Hall, *The Trinity* (Grand Rapids: Eerdmans, 2002), 113.

15. John Zizioulas, *Being as Communion: Studies in Personhood and the Church* (Crestwood, N.Y.: Saint Vladimir's Seminary Press, 1985), 15.

16. Alan Torrance, *Persons in Communion: An Essay on Trinitarian Description and Human Participation* (Edinburgh: T and T Clark, 1996), 288.

17. Miroslav Volf, *After Our Likeness: The Church as the Image of the Trinity* (Grand Rapids: Eerdmans, 1998), 172.

18. David Cunningham, *These Three Are One: The Practice of Trinitarian Theology* (Oxford: Blackwell, 1998), 26-30.

19. Volf, *After Our Likeness*, 11. See also Olson and Hall, *The Trinity*, 115; Colin Gunton, *The Promise of Trinitarian Theology* (2d ed.; Edinburgh: T and T Clark, 1993), 69, 226-7; and Cunningham, *These Three*, 170.

20. Paul Fiddes, *Participating in God: A Pastoral Doctrine of the Trinity* (London: DLT, 2000), 52.

21. Athanasius, *On the Incarnation*, trans. and ed. by a Religious of C.S.M.V. (Crestwood: St Vladimir's Seminary Press, 1996).

22. Athanasius, *On the Incarnation of the Word* 54, trans. Archibald Robertson (Nicene and Post Nicene Fathers 2/4; Grand Rapids, Eerdmans, 1978), 65.

23. Gordon D. Fee, *God's Empowering Presence: The Holy Spirit in the Letters of Paul* (Peabody: Hendrickson, 1994), 3.

24. Douglas Cambell, *Do Pauline Theology and Apocalyptic Belong Together?* (unpublished paper, 2002), 9.

25. See C. K. Barrett, *Commentary on the Second Epistle to the Corinthians* (New York: Harper and Row, 1973), 117.

26. Jervell, *Imago Dei*, quoted in Barrett, *Commentary*, 132.

27. Fee, *Gods's Empowering Presence*, 309.

28. John Chrysostom, *Homilies on Second Corinthians* 7.5 (Nicene and Post Nicene Fathers 1/12; Grand Rapids: Eerdmans, 1978), 314.

29. John Calvin, *Commentary on II Corinthians, Timothy, Titus and Philemon*, (Grand Rapids: Eerdmans 1948), 50.

30. Karl Barth, *Church Dogmatics* 3/1 (Edinburgh: T and T Clark, 1958), 204.

31. Philip Hughes, *Paul's Second Epistle to the Corinthians* (Grand Rapids: Eerdmans, 1962), 117.

32. Michael Ramsey, *The Glory of God and the Transfiguration of Christ* (London: Longmans, Green, 1949), 83.

33. See Pete Ward, *Liquid Church* (Carlisle: Paternoster, 1996).

Dr. Pete Ward is senior lecturer in youth ministry and theological education at King's College London. He is the author of Liquid Church *and* Selling Worship, *published by Hendrickson.*

Poetry as the Thing Itself

MARTHA SERPAS

I write poems set in my Southern Louisiana home, eighty miles south-southwest of New Orleans in Lafourche Parish, a small town called Galliano. Cajun country, settled by diverse peoples—Acadians, Houma Indians, Germans, Italians, and scores of others—has produced original, syncretic architecture, cuisine, music, language, art, and dance. Before the aftermath of Hurricane Katrina, I might have had to explain why I could very well outlive my hometown, how the land has been disintegrating. Now most people are aware of the devastating effects of pollution, poor planning, and oil industry dredging on Louisiana's coast. The Gulf is eating my home state so fast—twenty-five to forty-five square miles a year—that future generations will never know the communities where I grew up. Southern Louisiana is the fastest disappearing landmass in the world.

Environmentalists will tell you about the impact on migrating birds and other marsh-land inhabitants. "Eat all the crab you can now," because most so-called Maryland crabs come from Louisiana, and the crab industry is facing extinction. A third of domestic oil flows through Port Fourchon, threatened and sinking. A few miles from the port is a bridge, and from that bridge, no higher than a hill, one can get a fairly long view across the flat marsh. Nearby lakes, just twenty years ago, were land. The remains of a cemetery are dropping into the brackish water one cement vault at a time. Gray crosses and gaping holes where bodies were exhumed are visible at low tide.

These are the subjects of my poetry, and poetry and theology for me are correlatives. The disintegrating land that I describe is indistin-guishable from other disappearances—of the physical body, of ego, of faith, of certainties, of community.

Poetry and theology are both beholden to the physical world and strive to transcend it. They also are the victims of similar critiques: they are judged unreadable, abstruse, pedantic, out-of-touch. Often the same damning label is used—hopelessly *academic*. Those adjectives de-scribe poor theology and failed poems. Without an engaged audience, either pursuit is reduced to the private musings of a single mind. The mind *is* a friend to poetry and theology, but is not the primary source of either. Poetry and theology must share a partner in their enterprises, and that partner is the audience or reader. The audi-ence is intrinsic to the poetic and theological event, a co-creator of the thing itself.

Prayer, writes Simone Weil, is absolute unmixed attention—and so is poetry. Both are joyfully and grievously in-the-moment, all-con-suming, and both direct the heart to the Word. The Word is the *means* to the Divine end and the Divine itself. The Word is not a signifier but the thing proper: it is both vehicle and tenor at once.

Passion for language is a creative force in both poetic and theological endeavors. We are inescapably embodied and indebted to our senses; to convey any experience is to rely on sensory description. Poetry, I believe, can help theology avoid the graves of cliché and old meta-phors. Fixation on any image or fixture as an end in itself is idolatrous and reminds us why *grave* and *graven* have similar roots.

Poetry is fluid, ready to accept a new rhythm and a better phrase if either will fur-ther the cause of precision. The poet (and the theologian) trusts in a guiding Truth beyond her volition. As Richard Hugo writes, "You owe reality nothing, and the truth of your feelings ev-erything." For our purposes, I would offer, "This reality is not what the theologically minded poet is struggling to reach."

Poetry strives for the clearest, most specific image. Poetry knows that metaphor is not a lesser reality, a poor substitute—as in "oh, that's just a metaphor"—but points beyond an accessible reality to a greater Truth. Paradoxically, poetry is considered fiction. Certainly, poetry is a made thing, an invention, yes, but hardly without verity. Metaphor alone can offer us some approach to the Divine, and again, paradoxically, metaphor can never fully convey the Divine. Still, it remains our best bet.

In this way, poetry is sacramental. I await a book by Scott Cairns, a Greek Orthodox poet, on this subject. He has addressed the transubstantiated nature of poetry with great eloquence. Poetry does not represent; it is not a symbol. Poetry does not explain, and it does not point or show. Poetry does not exist to depict the thing; it is the thing itself. Its power is conjured between the audience and the poet.

Poetry is mysterious and respectful of silence. Without silence there is no music, and without music there is no poetry. Poetry is composed, after all. Poetry is shaped; poetry sings. It owes more to music and to sculpture than to prose writing. For me there is no possibility of untangling the poetic and theological impulse. Their vibrancy rests in the imagination, and they both call us to rest in the imagination, not as an escape, but as a return home.

In my poetry, I have borrowed from Simone Weil's writings on decreation. I use the dissolution of the land as metaphor for the dismantling of the self, which, for Weil, is a necessary suffering to achieve union with the Divine. Because, despite my impulse to educate and urge change, I am an elegist. What I praise is already gone.

The land and the people in my poems serve as vehicles for theological longing and suffering: tragic destruction is required for new creation. I try to conjure my home's sounds and colors in the immediacy they still hold for me, a present-tense paradox of abundance and loss existing in the same time and space, not a representation of a part of the temporal world, but a transformed reality.

Reburial at Sea

Leeville Cemetery, LA
They must have heard it coming—
the relentless marsh water
throwing itself against their vaults,
salt-heavy and exhausted, day
after day, the old bricks
warmed in the noon sun.
It must have sounded like regret, like
a bunkmate's throaty breathing
getting louder and closer
as the deckhands roll from sleep.
It must have set the marsh struggling,
high tide's long, muddy arms
that lift bodies into a bath
or onto the quilted Gulf.
It must have kept them company,
the persistent lapping, the slow rock
    down—
when one holds still, the world's
rough motions calm into shining ripples.
They must have been comforted
that change is possible for the dead.

Martha Serpas has published two collections of poetry, Côte Blanche *(New Issues, 2002) and* The Dirty Side of the Storm *(Norton, 2006). Her work has appeared or is forthcoming in* The New Yorker, The Nation, The Christian Century, *and* Image: A Journal of the Arts and Religion. *She was visiting professor of religion and literature at Yale Divinity School in fall 2005 and currently teaches at the University of Tampa, where she is an associate professor of English. She is co-poetry editor of* Tampa Review.

A Japanese Performance of Intertextuality:
From *Nô* to *Kabuki* to Film

BONNIE C. WADE

This paper resulted from the request by Professor Margot Fassler that I speak on a topic reflecting my research on the documentation of music history through visual sources. I responded that my research focused on sixteenth- and seventeenth-century Mughal miniature paintings (North India) that depict music and dance, but that recently I had returned to a focus on Japan. Would a visually-oriented paper on Japanese music be appropriate? Yes, she replied; the highly ritualized *nô* drama was of some interest at the Institute but familiar to few. Accordingly, the presentation was introductory and heavily laced with audio and visual material. To publish a cogent version of the text without that material is a challenge. What you read here is my attempt to retain to the extent possible the style and flow of such a scholarly production, as I develop the point that, from early instances of recorded poetry to theatrical forms to popular culture of the present day, creative Japanese, including musicians and other performing artists, have pursued "the intertextual effort" with relish. I take "intertextual effort" to mean "the complex and variegated play of borrowing, citation, implicit or explicit references…and substitutions, which substantiate the relationships between the texts of a given culture (and even between texts of different cultures)."[1]

The intertextual examples on which I focus are both verbal and musical. They have to do with a story, a play, and three different musical-dramatic enactments of that play that traverse five centuries of Japanese cultural production. I will explore three points about this particular intertextual effort: (1) in terms of mode, it utilizes both citation and reference; (2) in terms of intention, it is both meaningful and functional; and (3) its use had to be balanced with the need for relevance for each contemporary audience.

The story that underlies my illustrative example of the intertextual effort is a very old one with a basis in factual Japanese history, at least in terms of the main characters and the relationships among them, as well as some of their deeds and the broad outlines of events. The story transports us to medieval Japan of the twelfth century C.E. By that time centuries of a governmental system in which power and authority rested with an imperial establishment were drawing to a close with several decades of epic struggle between two clans—the Heike and the Genji—for controlling power. The Genji clan, and specifically the Minamoto family within that clan, emerged victorious, and a new form of governance was instituted in which power resided with the *samurai* (warrior) class, while titular authority—such as it was—remained with the person of the Emperor. That system, initiated officially as the Kamakura Shogunate (1185-1333) by Yoritomo Minamoto, remained in place until the mid-nineteenth century, though the *samurai* clan in control changed several times. Stories of the twelfth-century struggle abounded and have survived, indeed flourished, in forms oral and literary; needless to say, they constitute much material from which artists have drawn for the practice of intertextuality—a deeply enculturated Japanese practice.

"Ataka" in the Nô *Style*

I will demonstrate this through a play that is based more or less on an episode in the epic *Tale of the Heike*. The play, "Ataka," was fashioned for enactment in the style of the *nô* theater by the playwright Nobumitsu Kojiro (1435-1516), a playwright member of the Kanze lineage of hereditary actors.[2] By his time the story was already an old one, told in various forms,[3] but the *nô* drama style was still relatively recent; it was developed by the actor-theorist Motokiyo

Zeami (1363?–1443?), whose lifetime probably overlapped with Kojiro's.

The aesthetics of the *nô* style lie primarily in Zen Buddhism owing to the patronage of Zeami by the third head of the Ashikaga clan of *samurai* which was then in control of the country (1336-1573). (Of the numerous sects of Buddhism in Japan, the sect of the highest-ranking *samurai* was Zen.) The Zen aesthetic expresses at once elegance and a striving for simplicity. Drawing on existing dance, music, and theatrical forms in good intertextual manner, Zeami created an intricate fusion of music, dance, mask, costume, and language.[4] His *nô* performing style was specifically associated with the elite level of *samurai* society. Because *nô* has been transmitted very carefully from the medieval period, one can assume when watching a live or filmed contemporary performance that one is witnessing a very old form of dramatic production. *Nô* retains its elite cultural status to the present time.

In the *nô* performing style the aesthetic principle of "maximum effect from a minimum of means" is manifested in many ways. Originally (and occasionally still) presented in a small wooden pavilion on temple grounds, *nô* is now most often presented in such a pavilion that has been constructed inside a theater. Open on two sides to the audience, the relatively small, highly polished wooden stage is connected to the green room by a walkway that is utilized dramatically; the pavilion's tiled roof covers them both. The stage backdrop is always a single pine tree painted on the rear wall. Theatrical props are kept to a minimum; lighting remains consistent. The acting is suggestive rather than realistic, each motion so stylized, so slow, and pared to such a minimum that it creates a tremendous effect. Sliding their feet, with their bodies held in a certain stance, actors glide for the most part rather than walk or run. Dance segments of the plays seem hardly that. Actors (only male) sing as well as speak and dance; they are few in number, categorized as role types. A male chorus sits to stage right; two (or three) drummers and a flutist line

up across the stage at the rear. Only the brocaded silk costumes are rich and elaborate, reminders of the wealth of *nô*'s medieval patrons.

The plays, too, are relatively simple. In essence, "Ataka" is about the *samurai* code of loyalty to one's superior even in the most difficult of circumstances.[5] Yoritomo Minamoto has emerged from the Genji-Heike struggles as the most powerful individual in Japan. Unfortunately, in 1187 a desperate internecine struggle ensues between him and his younger brother Yoshitsune, a lieutenant (a *hôgan*) who had stood with him in many battles. Now Yoritomo has turned against his brother. Sorrowfully, Yoshitsune flees from the capital, forced on the orders of his brother to take a dangerous route over a mountain pass that is guarded by a military barrier.

Yoshitsune is a brave, heroic person of the *samurai* class; he is also elegant and courtly of manner as a person of his elite status would have been. (Interestingly, in "Ataka" he is usually played by a child actor, suggesting perhaps the powerless circumstances to which he has been reduced.) Fleeing with him is Benkei, his loyal retainer-warrior, who devises a plan by which they and their small band of men try to get through the barrier. Although they have a porter (a baggage carrier, *gôriki*) in their band, they disguise Yoshitsune as a lowly porter as well. Benkei and the rest of the *samurai* don the robes of traveling mountain monks (*yamabushi*, as they were called, were real characters of considerable interest in the medieval period) who pretend to be collecting funds to rebuild an important Buddhist temple in the capital that has been destroyed in the fighting between the clans. A rumor circulates about this disguise, however, and it has reached the ears of Togashi, the high-ranking officer who, with another group of *samurai*, is guarding the mountain pass through which Benkei and his men must pass. Togashi has ordered that any *yamabushi* who come to the barrier be summarily executed. Indeed, some have been already; returning from scouting, the real baggage carrier reports seeing heads on stakes.

Benkei's encounter with Togashi constitutes the centerpiece of the story. Even though Benkei tries to persuade Togashi that they are real monks on this fundraising project, Togashi tells the group that they must prepare to meet their fate. Observing a ritual within the play, they proceed with "final offices" appropriate to their Buddhist faith. But then Togashi decides to pursue the matter of the fundraising project, and demands that Benkei read his official charge from the subscription document (*kanjinchô*) that he must be carrying from the temple, and on which he will write the names of donors. Pretending that he really has a *kanjinchô*, and standing at an angle that prevents Togashi's seeing it, Benkei "reads" dramatically from an empty scroll. So effective is Benkei that Togashi is letting the men go—until a barrier guard thinks he recognizes Yoshitsune in the disguised porter and they are again stopped.

This is the crucial moment of the story: the only way Benkei can convince Togashi that Yoshitsune is not Yoshitsune is to commit an act unforgivable in the *samurai* code. Ignoring the order to stop, he "accuses" the porter of not moving quickly enough, and beats his lord and master, shouting "Pass on!" Togashi has become convinced that Yoshitsune is indeed Yoshitsune, but he so admires Benkei for taking the potentially self-destructive risk he has taken to save his master that he decides to let them go. He even pledges a gift for the rebuilding of the Todaiji temple. Thus the band passes through the barrier.

Once they are away, Benkei apologizes, Yoshitsune forgives him, and we think the story is ending. But here comes the offer of a gift of *sake* wine which Togashi sends to redeem his rudeness to Benkei. A drinking scene ensues, complete with the enjoyment of "spontaneous" dance. Fortunately, inebriation does not result in tragic indiscretion. The play ends with the men feeling that they have "stepped on a tiger's tail" but escaped.

"Ataka" in Kabuki and Film

When Nobumitsu Kojiro wrote this play Yoshitsune and Benkei were the stuff of very lively legends-in-the-making, the shogunate system of government was showing prospects for keeping peace in the land, and a social system with a privileged *samurai* class was being worked out. About three hundred years later, however, the shogunate under the extremely powerful Tokugawa clan (1600-1868) had become extremely oppressive. Japanese society was highly segmented, and the *samurai* class was so huge, privileged, and uncontrollable, that rebellion was afoot. It was at that time that "Ataka" was transformed into a play for performance in *kabuki* theater style by the playwright Namiki Gohei III (1789–1855). This version of the play was called "Kanjinchô" in reference to the subscription scroll.

The *kabuki* theater was a lively part of urban life in the Tokugawa capital, Edo (now Tokyo). The government attempted to control it, confining theaters and, to a large extent, even the actors to the pleasure districts outside the city proper.[6] Much of the content of *kabuki* entertainment comprised titillatingly sensual dance pieces performed by the male actors, and plays about the lives of the common people, including the courtesans of the pleasure quarters. There were some historical plays from the old epics, and plays adapted from the established and stable *nô* drama repertoire.

Still, adapting "Ataka"—a play without any female characters, and deeply expressive of religious philosophy—for the popular *kabuki* theater after three hundred years seems to me a choice worthy of interrogation. Because I agree that intertextual practice is in various ways functional, I cannot help but ruminate on the reasons. Perhaps it was brought into the repertoire to appeal to the elite members of the audience; there will have been some. But perhaps there was some more political reason: government pressure on the *kabuki* producers to remind the *samurai* in the audience of higher ideals of their class than they were then upholding, or, through the play's theme of loyalty, to advocate for loyalty to the Tokugawa while their establishment was having increasing difficulty maintaining control. Or, conversely, perhaps it was a covert way on the part of the "artistic world" to encourage those *samurai* serving in rebelling groups to act loyally to their leaders. I have yet to find explanations in the work of Japanese literary historians.

What leads me to posit possible political motivations is the third appearance of the play "Ataka" in dramatized form: in 1945, when the war effort was utterly desperate in Japan, "Ataka" was adapted by the director Akira Kurosawa as a feature film for the government-controlled wartime movie industry. The title of that version, "Tora no o fumu otokotachi" ("Men Who Step on the Tiger's Tail") was taken from the penultimate line of "Ataka."

> Tora no o o fumi
> dokuja no kuchi o
> nogaretaru kokochi shite.

> Stepping on the tiger's tail
> they all feel as though they go
> escaping from the serpent's poison jaw.

For the movie industry to have drawn on a traditional theatrical form was not in the least unusual. The film historian Darrell Davis describes a set of films made from the late 1930s through the war as in "monumental style because they invest a form of spirituality in traditional Japanese heritage. . . . The films enact a canonization of history, an emphasis on indigenous art forms and design, and a corresponding technical repertoire of long takes and long shots, very slow camera movements, and a highly ceremonial manner of blocking, acting and set design. The monumental style sets out to transform Japanese tradition from a cultural legacy into a sacrament."[7]

Although that description of the style evokes images of *nô* drama performance, the traditional theater from which filmmakers drew most was *kabuki*, and therefore the historical period most invoked was the Tokugawa era with its heroic *samurai bushido* code.

"Men Who Step on the Tiger's Tail" is an exceptional film in many ways, not the least of which is its setting in the pre-Tokugawa period, an even more idealized time. And, rather than violence and bravado, there is quiet, strong courage. I think of a ritual within the play that is retained fully in the film—the Buddhist rite by which Benkei, Yoshitsune, and their small band of men prepare themselves for death. How very meaningful, how relevant the story must have been at that desperate time when Tokyo was in ruins from firebombing and the war's end in defeat was imminent. The play was potentially a powerful means of invoking in the suffering populace the ideals the government was depending on—courage and loyalty in the face of even the most difficult circumstances.

While the story of the crossing of the barrier could have been retold in film entirely without citations from the text and references to the stylistic content of the *nô* play "Ataka," Kurosawa made it a deeply intertextual dramatic production. The story's potency for its audience would have been all the greater through the stylistic invocation of that particular vignette from history, by those textual reminders of traditional practices, by nostalgic re-enactment of idealized ways of being and thinking in the *nô* style, whose "sacramental gravity remains inviolate."[8] The layers of meaning were not lost on the censorship board of the American Occupation Forces, who banned the showing of the just-completed film.

Intertextuality in Variant Versions of "Ataka"

In subsequent productions there have been some differences in both poetry and prose from the original "Ataka." As one would expect, the differences are greater as the medium moves from *nô* to *kabuki* and then to film. Some of the liberties in the *kabuki* and film versions are those taken when a novel is adapted to film — characters added, perspectives shifted, some segments emphasized and others downplayed or omitted. The only example I will mention concerns the character of the baggage carrier. As recounted above, in the *nô* play there is a servant porter (*gôriki*) in the original small band of men; in the play his one task is to act as a scout near the barrier and to report back to Benkei. In the *kabuki* version the *gôriki* has no function; he is merely on stage. In the film, however, the *gôriki* is a character with a real role. He has been hired locally and is acting informally as a guide. At first the lowly porter has no idea who the men are, and his relationship with them as events unfold is part of the interest of the film version. Kurosawa, who was clearly familiar with the *nô* drama tradition, knew of the comic role type called *kyôgen*. In intertextual fashion he combined the possibility of a comic *kyôgen* role in *nô* with the actuality of the porter character in "Ataka" to create a major purveyor of drama and levity in the film. For instance, twentieth-century filmgoers unfamiliar with the old story can realize from the panicked reaction of the *gôriki* that Benkei "reads" to Togashi from an empty scroll.

As for the music in these dramatic productions, one element links *nô* and *kabuki*: the ensemble of four instrumentalists, three drummers and a flutist. Coordinated vocal calls by the drummers, and the sounds of their interlocking drumming patterns, add considerably to the drama. They are basic to all music of the *nô* and to some of the *kabuki* musical genres. For "Kanjinchô" as for "Ataka," they are arrayed in full view across the rear of the stage.

However, in *kabuki* and film the music too moves farther and farther from that of the *nô*. Most important in this regard is the place of music in the particular dramatic medium. As with opera, music is integral to the *nô* performing style; without music, *nô* would not be *nô*. Actors are singers, and the chorus members are members of the troupe who are not playing a role on a given day. For *kabuki*, however, music is not a defining feature of the performance ilk as a whole. Some *kabuki* plays include no music; in many off-stage musicians provide musical intertextual references that complement the stage text and action — the sound of an ominously, slowly beaten temple bell that the audience understands as suggestive of impending doom, or a moment of festival music on flute and percussion to suggest a celebration and fun. On the other hand, some plays feature musical scenes, while others are musical throughout. All singing is done by specialist musicians. When a *nô* play is adapted to *kabuki*, the music integral to the play will be maintained — in its place, but not the same music necessarily, nor the expectation that the actors will do the singing.

As for films, we expect music in the course of most of them, and it can certainly fulfill dramatic purposes. However, music is generally kept very much in the background, functioning almost subliminally. The music for "Men Who Step on the Tiger's Tail" lies somewhere between that subliminality and its place in *kabuki*: as is intended for *kabuki* audiences, I think we are supposed to be mindful of the music — or at least the soundscape — a good deal of the time. Intertextual references abound, and texted song in the film functions much as the chorus parts do in *nô* drama.

Music also moves progressively farther from *nô* in content and style. This, too, has to do with the particular performing medium. Also, I think it has to do with the aesthetic expectations of the audience. In the *nô* performing style text is rendered as heightened speech (*kotoba*), or is set to melody (*fushi*) in one of two styles. One of these (*yowagin*) is true melodic singing, but of a very stylized sort: it has three central pitches — low, middle, and high — and the singer moves certain ways among them. The other style of melody (*tsuyogin*), more like chant than "melody," reveals the influence of Buddhist chant.[9]

To a greater extent than in most *nô* plays the text in "Ataka" is rendered either in heightened speech or in the chant-like style. The nature of the story—ostensibly being about monks on a religious mission—might be the reason.

This ponderous vocal style would not have appealed to the audience for *kabuki*. *Kabuki* belonged to the realm of popular culture, with lyrical songs. No clearer sign of popular culture exists than the *shamisen*—the long-necked plucked lute used to accompany professional singers. The *shamisen* was an instrument of urban popular music par excellence, a world away from the aesthetic of the *nô* drama. In "Kanjinchô" an equal number of singers and *shamisen* players sit arrayed at the rear of the stage, elevated on a riser behind the percussionists and flutist.

With such differences between the musical content and styles of *nô* and *kabuki*, the question arises of what happened musically when a play from the former repertoire was performed as the latter, and more specifically, when "Ataka" was performed as "Kanjinchô"? Because *kabuki* developed in a period when Japanese society was highly segmented, *nô* plays could be adapted into *kabuki*, but personnel did not move with them. Musicians of the *nô* drama world were not likely to intersect with professional musicians in the *kabuki* music world. The singers of *kabuki* music did not study the acting roles or the chorus parts of *nô* plays, and *nô* actors would not study the singing of the *kabuki* music styles; they inhabited separate socio-cultural spaces.

That being the case, we are led to consider those moments in "Kanjinchô" when the *nô* style of vocal delivery was cited. As one would expect, this occurred at crucial moments, including, for instance, Benkei's weighty pretense of reading from the subscription scroll. At the beginning and end of the play, too, the memory of *nô* is invoked not only through text but also through the vocal delivery.[10]

The play begins, as all *nô* plays begin, with the second-most important character (*waki*) introducing himself. In "Ataka" that is Togashi:

we see him giving orders to the barrier guards to be on the lookout for mountain monks. Then comes another standard segment: the entrance of the most important character (*shite*)—in this case Benkei—to ensemble entry music, followed by an expressive poem sung in the chant-like vocal style by the chorus. The drummers' calls and strokes are also very expressive here. The poem is in classical form, with lines in the syllable pattern of seven plus five (first line repeated). (The "n" of shioruran counts as a syllable.)

> *Suzukake no Tabi no koromo wa*
> *tsuyukeki sode ya*
> *shioruran.*

> Dressed in the traveling robes of monks,
> sweeping the dew,
> our sleeves are drenched.

In the *nô* play Benkei and his men proceed to review their journey; they explain that their Lord Benkei is disguised as chief among the monks, and they are setting out again on their difficult journey. *Nô* plays always begin with someone traveling somewhere—geographically, or perhaps psychologically. This exchange is omitted in the *kabuki* play.

Benkei and his men then set the scene in terms of time, place, and feeling in text that is retained in the *kabuki*. This text is poetry also, and it permits me to point out another instance of intertextuality: Embedded within a longer newly-composed passage are these lines from a pre-existent poem that the medieval playwright cited:

> *Kore ya kono*
> *yuku mo kaeru mo*
> *Wakarete wa*
> *shiru mo shiranu mo*

> Oh, there lies the Hill of Meeting
> where travelers who come and go,
> both friends and strangers,
> though once parted, shall ever meet again.

In the *nô* play the singing style is still the chant-like melody, at a higher pitch. The drums continue to play in close coordination with the singing.

In *kabuki* the intertextual use of the *nô* text of the opening poem, and the scene-setting poem, is literal citation; however, the music is referential. The instrumental entry music at the beginning is imitative of *nô* but not adopted precisely. It properly begins with a shrill flute blast that unmistakably announces this moment in the play; also properly, the drums start out with an approximation of the *nô* patterns. The singers render the opening poem of "Ataka" with "choral" chant-like vocal delivery, accompanied on drums by an imitation of the *nô* pattern. However, that quickly gives way to a declaration that this is *kabuki*, with the entry of the popular-culture *shamisen*. The text is again cited from the *nô* play, but the music has become *kabuki* music—a song genre called *nagauta*.[11]

What happens in the Kurosawa film here at the beginning? The small band of "monks" in familiar robes are on their way somewhere as in the *nô* play. True to the story, they are making their way on a mountain trail. We hear bells in the distance, suggesting the many temples the men would have been passing in the old Heike stories. Most telling in intertextual terms, we also hear the opening poem, albeit from an unseen chorus of male singers. Significantly, the chorus starts out in chant-like style, as in *nô*. The first twelve syllables are sung only once, however, and by the second line of the poem the intertextual reference is pared to only the text. The music is made more relevant to the film's audience in two ways: by substituting for the ponderous *nô*-style melody the lush male choral sound that was widespread in Japan at the time the film was made, and by an orchestral accompaniment to the chorus. By the middle of the twentieth century Western music was the preeminent music of Japanese culture, and an orchestra was likely to be providing music for films. As the play was

taken from *nô* to *kabuki* to film, then, the music also moved farther and farther away from *nô*.

These examples have shown how, at the macroscopic level, the story of Yoshitsune and Benkei at the Ataka barrier—a vignette drawn from epic history—has provided material for considerable intertextual effort. Down a level of specificity, one particular dramatized version—the *nô* play "Ataka"—has been used meaningfully for two other dramatic productions. At a more microscopic level, pieces of the text of "Ataka" and moments of its music have been cited or suggested in purposeful ways.

Though to adapt a play that was created originally for some other style of dramatic production for *kabuki* was commonplace, it seems reasonable to raise the possibility that the adaptation of "Ataka" to *kabuki* three hundred years after its creation served some political purpose. Likewise, adhering as closely as the film did to the *nô* play transported the weightiest of dramatic traditions into the contemporary medium of film at a very serious time in Japanese history. The practice of intertextuality in these examples was intellectual, aesthetic, and functional on the part of playwrights, musicians, and a film director.

For an intertextual effort to be effective, it must constitute a form of communication among those who share knowledge: audiences have to be cognizant that some text is being cited or suggested, and understand why. If they understand, the intertextual effort serves to reinforce cultural memory and also to deepen meaning. In the early fifteenth century when "Ataka" was written and enacted for its elite *samurai* audience, the degree of shared knowledge and understanding of meanings in the text and music could be counted upon to be great. When the play was adopted for *kabuki*, however, the degree of shared knowledge and understanding of the original text and performance style was probably not great. Thus, the new intertextual production did additional work: while communicating through shared knowledge and understanding to those in the audience who might know, it could also be a means of disseminating some old and new knowledge and understanding to a broader audience. Kurosawa's challenge was the greatest: his introduction of the comic character, I think, gave him a mediator, a kind of translator for modern reception.

Among Japanese audiences at the beginning of the twenty-first century, cultural memory of the story and of the "Kanjinchô" version is lively. It is the canonic piece from the *kabuki* repertoire that school children learn about, in the little they learn about their traditional culture. Theatrical productions are presented regularly. A sense of its present life can be gained by an internet search under "Kanjinchô." There it is, material for new intertextual effort.[12]

ENDNOTES

1. Marco DeMarinis, *The Semiotics of Performance*, trans. Aine O'Healy (Bloomington: Indiana University Press, 1993), 4.

2. "Ataka," in *Masterworks of the Nô Theater*, trans. Kenneth Yasuda (Bloomington: Indiana University Press, 1989).

3. See *The Tale of the Heike*, trans. Helen Craig McCullough (Stanford: Stanford University Press, 1988).

4. See Kunio Komparu, *The Noh Theater: Principles and Perspectives* (New York: Weatherhill, 1983).

5. See *Yoshitsune: A Fifteenth-Century Japanese Chronicle*, trans. Helen Craig McCullough (Stanford: Stanford University Press, 1971, 1990).

6. See Donald Shively, "Bakufu versus Kabuki." *Harvard Journal of Asian Studies* 18 (1955): 326-56; "The Social Environment of Tokugawa Kabuki," in *Studies in Kabuki: Its Acting, Music, and Historical Context*, ed. James Brandon et al. (Honolulu: University Press of Hawaii, 1978), 1-61.

7. Darrell William Davis, *Picturing Japaneseness: Monumental Style, National Identitiy, Japanese Film* (New York: Columbia University Press, 1996), 2 and 6.

8. Davis, *Picturing Japaneseness*, 109.

9. These styles are illustrated in my book *Music in Japan: Experiencing Music, Expressing Culture* (New York: Oxford University Press, 2005), with CD.

10. For the texts, see my *Music in Japan*. In the oral presentation at Yale comparisons of these moments were made with audio and video clips.

11. See James R. Brandon et al., eds., *Studies in Kabuki: Its Acting, Music, and Historical Context* (Honolulu: University Press of Hawaii, 1978).

12. For further information on this subject see *Traditional Japanese Theater: An Anthology of Plays*, ed. Karen Brazell (New York: Columbia University Press, 1998); "The Tradition of Performing Arts in Japan: The Artistry of Kabuki, Noh, and Bunraku," in the series *Japan: The Land and Its People*, produced by Shin-Ei, Inc. 1989. VHS. 29 min. Distributed by GPN, P.O.Box 80669, Lincoln, NE 68501-0669 (gpn@unlinfo.unl.edu).

———————————

Bonnie C. Wade, past president of the Society for Ethnomusicology, is the Richard and Rhoda Goldman Distinguished Chair in Interdisciplinary Studies and professor of ethnomusicology at the University of California, Berkeley. A specialist in the music of India and Japan, she is the author of several books, the most recent being Imaging Sound: An Ethnomusicological Study of Music, Art, and Culture in Mughal India *(University of Chicago Press, 1998),* Thinking Musically *(Oxford University Press, 2004), and* Music in Japan: Experiencing Music, Expressing Culture *(Oxford University Press, 2005). She is co-general editor of the Oxford University Press Global Music Series and also is presently serving as chair of the Department of Music and of the Group in Asian Studies at Berkeley.*

Eastern Liturgy in the West: The Case of the Armenian Church

MICHAEL DANIEL FINDIKYAN

I am not a specialist in the field of inculturation, so what I offer you is not at all a scholarly address; I will not in any way claim to be comprehensive or definitive in my remarks. That leaves me free to ruminate and to reflect with you on the topic at hand without the obligation to be systematic, or even to tie up loose ends. I shall speak to the topic of inculturation as a student of the history of liturgy and as a representative of the Christian East, specifically as a priest of the Armenian Orthodox Church, and as a practitioner of the Armenian Rite. My hope is that my remarks will leave many threads for you to pick at during our discussion later.

Let our ruminations begin, therefore, with a bit of background for the purpose of contextualization. The Armenian Church is one of the so-called Oriental Orthodox Churches. Along with the Coptic, Ethiopian, Syrian ("Jacobite"), and Malankara Orthodox Churches, the Armenian Church is distinguished from the other Orthodox Churches (Greek, Russian, and so on) by its Christology, that is, by its rejection of the Fourth Ecumenical Council of Chalcedon and its particular formulation for understanding the humanity and divinity of Jesus Christ. In liturgical rite, history, and spirituality, however, the Oriental Orthodox Churches are actually quite distinct one from the other.[1] Today the Armenian Rite is used or practiced by an estimated six million faithful of the Armenian Church, as well as approximately three hundred forty-four thousand members of the Armenian Catholic Church in communion with Rome.

What we call the Armenian Rite is a complete and integrated system of worship; a unique synthesis of liturgical usages and practices that expresses the instinctive, traditional response of the Armenian people to God's providential activity in history. That history begins with the Bible, of course. Medieval Armenian historians have traditionally viewed the history of the Armenian people in direct continuity with the Bible.[2] Since the proclamation of Christianity as the state religion in the early fourth century, Armenian historiographers have systematically and unapologetically interpreted their own unfolding history in light of their faith in Christ. Until the eighteenth century there simply is no such thing as Armenian secular history.

The Armenian Rite is a system of common prayer, that is, prayer for the community, composed, collated, and utilized *by* the Armenian people *for* the Armenian people, having its own distinctive inner logic and perspective.[3] This system of worship includes not only the Divine Liturgy but also the services traditionally conducted each day—morning prayers, evening prayers, Compline prayers at bedtime, a unique and beautiful daily Sunrise Service, and various forms of all-night vigils.[4] The rite includes the sacraments, which for us Armenians are traditionally not limited to seven, as they are in the West, but include blessings for the sick, a variety of very poignant penitential services, as well as all kinds of other liturgical ceremonies like funerals, the consecration of a church, the blessing of water, footwashing on Holy Thursday, the blessing of grapes, and many others.

Moreover, the liturgical Rite of the Armenian Church, properly speaking, is not even limited to church services. It comprises the texts of the prayers and hymns in all of their theological and poetic splendor; the system of organizing these liturgical texts for certain days; the selection and arrangement of church feasts throughout what is called the liturgical year; the cycle of saints' commemorations; the lectionary; even the vestments worn by bishops, priests, deacons, and altar servers. The liturgical Rite of the Armenians goes on to include the peculiar melodic patterns of sacred music, and even the architectural structure of the church building and the sacred art that adorns it. After all, the church edifice must be designed to accommodate the liturgical services and rituals that take place within its walls (and not infrequently outside as well). All of this constitutes the Armenian Rite. Its rituals, prayers, hymns, and underlying theology are inextricably linked to the history, culture, and distinctive theological perspective of the Armenian people. The liturgy of the Armenian Church, in other words, expresses how the Armenian people have experienced and understood the Christian faith throughout the centuries.

The renowned specialist of Eastern Christian worship, my teacher Robert Taft, S.J., has expressed the role of liturgy in the Eastern Christian churches in these rhapsodic terms:

> The key to the heart of the Christian East is its liturgy . . . It is only through the liturgy that Scripture, tradition, the Fathers, piety, spirituality—everything—is transmitted and lived. Sometimes . . . this expression of a living faith can become sclerotic, overgrown, too heavy. But underneath the overgrowth of centuries lie the jewels of a people's incarnation of the gospel, waiting to be uncovered by someone willing to cut back the brush. I cannot imagine a more fitting, immensely rewarding ministry than to study the heritage of a people—and in the East that heritage is conserved and transmitted through the liturgy—in order to uncover its riches for the good of that same people, and of all peoples, to the unending glory of God's eternal name.[5]

It is uniquely in its liturgy, therefore, that a Christian community's particular experience of the Christian faith—in other words, its distinctive witness to Christ's Gospel—is to be found. This is particularly relevant to Eastern Christian communities, and it is certainly true for the ancient Christian faith of the Armenian people.

How do the Armenians understand the Gospel of Jesus Christ? What does Christ's resurrection mean to the Armenians? What aspects of the Christian faith do Armenians consider particularly evocative? The liturgy of the Armenian Church reveals how the Armenians have believed in God, how an ancient people, mercilessly oppressed and persecuted for most of its existence, rooted its identity in Christian faith, not as some inert cultural manifestation or transient philosophical movement, but as a life-giving, life-sustaining, life-defining reality.

Something more must be said about liturgy from an Eastern perspective. Liturgy in its fullest sense is simultaneously the means and the end of our Christian journey. All the churches of the Christian East share the conviction that the liturgy is more than common, corporate prayer. It is more than "the service of God offered by the people of God," as one theological dictionary puts it.[6] All of the Eastern churches share the belief that the liturgy is a genuine "participation" (*koinonia*) in the living Christ, to use St. Paul's terminology (1 Cor 10:16). In the prayers, psalms, hymns, and rituals of the sacraments and of the services of the Daily Cycle, and most conspicuously in the Eucharistic Liturgy, our salvation is actualized, and the church's true essence par excellence is manifested. The fathers of the Christian East rarely pass up the opportunity to avow that we actually experience Christ's redemptive work by conducting the elements of the liturgy. The psalms and canticles of the Morning Office, for example, work on us. As we sing and pray them, as those sacred words wash over us, the salvation effected by Christ unfolds for us. They put us in touch with the Saviour, and with Christ's redemptive acts in history. In the liturgy, Eastern and Oriental Orthodoxy insists, the "body" is joined to its "head" (Col 1:18, 2:19), to continue with St. Paul's imagery. If that is the case, then we can say that in our devotion to the liturgy, in our participation in the liturgy, we indeed grow in the Orthodox faith. We come to understand more deeply what the faith is all about. Consequently, in the Christian East we understand liturgy to be an exercise, a kind of nourishment, a sort of catechetical school, by the grace of the Holy Spirit.[7]

The late Orthodox theologian Alexander Schmemann expressed this idea deftly:

> Something happens in and through all these celebrations. Something happens not only in the Church but also in my life, in my life as an individual, as a member of a family, as a member of human society . . . something so beautiful, so heavenly, so crucial for real Orthodoxy that when we lose it — even though we can still build beautiful churches with domes and three-barred crosses and even know Orthodox melodies — we cease to be Orthodox.[8]

II.

Let's take a trip to Armenia. Allow me to lead you, via your imagination, on a visit to an Armenian Church in the old country. The church I have chosen is in the town of Etchmiadzin, about ten miles from Armenia's capital city of Yerevan, in the shadow of the biblical Mount Ararat. In this town the patron saint of the Armenian people, St. Gregory the Illuminator (or Baptizer) converted the pagan Armenian king, Drtad, to Christianity in the early years of the fourth century. Armenia thus became the first nation to proclaim Christianity as its official religion, some years before Emperor Constantine did the same for the Byzantine Empire, and several decades before the Christianization of the Empire actually took hold and became permanent. Around this time St. Gregory was bowed down in prayer in a field, when, in a vision, he saw Jesus Christ descend and mark the spot on which the first cathedral of Christendom would be built. Hence the name of the cathedral, and of the town, Etchmiadzin: "the place where the Only-begotten descended."[9]

But we are not going to visit the cathedral of Etchmiadzin. Follow me about a mile down the dusty road, in the same town, to another sacred edifice, the martyrium and church of St. Hripsimé. St. Hripsimé was a nun from Rome, who, together with some companions, fled to Armenia from the brutal persecution of Christians by the Emperor Diocletian. A beautiful young woman, she caught the eye of the Armenian king Drtad before his conversion by St. Gregory. When Hripsimé refused to yield to the pagan king's lascivious desires, he had her brutally tortured and killed, but not before the young maiden made a public profession of her faith in the risen Christ. Hripsimé died a martyr. Her earthly remains were gathered up by St. Gregory and her followers, and an unassuming church dedicated to her intercession was built over them.

The beautiful church that we are visiting today replaced the original one in the year A.D. 618, some fourteen hundred years ago. What strikes the eye first is the sheer enormousness of this edifice. With stone walls four feet thick, it exemplifies the major achievement of Armenian sacred architecture: the construction of massive, fortress-like churches that had to withstand not only the constant tremors of this seismically active region, but also the perpetual assaults inflicted by Armenia's bellicose neighbors. In the early period these were Persians and Arabs, later Seljuk Turks, Mamelukes, and Mongols.[10] Yet while standing tall and strong, the Church of St. Hripsimé radiates a delicate grace and beauty that echoes the young martyred maiden, and perhaps somehow exhibits the character and spirituality of Armenian Christianity.

It is early Sunday morning. Old, rotund women shrouded in black make their way around the perimeter of the church building. They pause at each face and kiss the cold stone walls of the church, raising their hands high and mumbling unintelligible entreaties as they make their way around the church in an ageless personal devotion. For these pious women Christianity is not an ideology. The Church is not a compartmentalized component of their lives to be reconciled with other pursuits and aspirations. Theirs is the real world. Their incentive is the selfsame shining ray of hope celebrated by the first pious women who went to the tomb to anoint Christ's body.

We step into the doorway on the rutted, dusty stone floor that has received a millennium-and-a-half of Armenian worshipers. A vast pillar-less space opens before us, crowned by an enormous conical dome that soars a hundred feet above. It is as if the sweeping dome envelops and embraces all who enter the church.

There are no pews. People move freely about the open worship space, their prostrations and ritual gestures unrestrained by furniture. Old and young, they gravitate toward alcoves tucked into the rear corners of the sanctuary. They are lured by the crackling of burning votive candles packed too tight into a crude, sand-filled candle-stand. A young mother offers her prayer to God while her child reaches to light his taper from flames leaping a foot above burning pools of melted beeswax.

Faint light flickering from the candles is absorbed by the cavernous space. It is dim, but not dark; grave, but not gloomy. Narrow openings sliced out of each face of the drum supporting the cupola allow only thin shafts of light to stream in. The medieval architect was also an astronomer; the narrow slits are positioned precisely to catch the light of the sun as it courses the daylight sky.

At the far end of the sanctuary, toward the East, rises the bema, a stage-like platform elevated four feet above the nave. This is the inner sanctuary, the holy of holies; on it the tiered altar table rests, the sacred space for the Eucharist. A lone, faded oriental rug in front of the altar table, the only floor-covering in the church, marks this holy ground where the priest offers the eucharistic sacrifice. The ministers who climb the steps up to the bema to the altar space first remove their shoes, like Moses.

But it is still very early on Sunday morning. The eucharistic liturgy has not yet begun.

The priest and the deacons, distributed in two choirs, stand in the chancel area before the elevated bema and conduct the early Morning Office, or, to translate more literally the Armenian, they "sing the hour." Sweet incense wafts upward, carrying prayers to God in an old and familiar fragrance that seizes the imagination of Armenians and invites them to a holy place.

Meanwhile, something similar is resonating in the airwaves. Open on a rickety podium in the chancel is a heavy book containing the well-traveled words of the Psalter. These words from the old Greek Septuagint were adopted by the Armenians and recast into their own language in the early fifth century, just months after a unique alphabet had been created for the express purpose of translating the Bible into Armenian. Generations of scribes have transmitted this version across the generations to be appropriated anew, to be sung and prayed.

Today our deacon in the church of St. Hripsimé once more transforms black ink on a page into the heartfelt, poignant prayer of his people by a musical-sacramental art as yet unknown to theorists and textbooks, yet practiced for centuries. In a quantum moment, our deacon scans the Armenian words of Psalm 118 (119), absorbs them, turns them in his mind and in his heart and in his imagination. Then he brings the words of the Psalm to life in music. The melody is not fixed and predetermined, nor is the deacon guided by the medieval Armenian pneumes printed above the psalm text; the art of deciphering these indigenous musical symbols was lost centuries ago, the victim of one of the periodic bouts of ethnic, intellectual, and cultural genocide perpetrated against the Armenians by various Turkic tribes during much of their history. Our deacon is guided, rather, by the conventional musical framework of one of the distinctive Armenian melodic modes of the *octoechos*. Within the limits set by convention and tradition, our deacon is free—indeed he is expected—to exploit the full musical potential of the given mode—melody, rhythm, ornamentation, dynamics, rubato, vocal effects — in order to interpret the words of the psalm, to give it a sacramental thrust as expressively and effectively as he can. What results is neither rote melody, nor merely words set to music, nor even mere psalmody, but a prayer whose words and spirit have been assumed and given impetus in music. Armenian hymnody is a kind of prayerful, musical exegesis.

What we have witnessed in the church of St. Hripsimé is a taste of the Armenian people's distinctive incarnation of the Gospel in their life and reality; a sample of that "something so beautiful, so heavenly, so crucial" that Schmemann envisions in the liturgy.

III.

As a result of the sad vicissitudes of Armenia's history, today more Armenians live outside their homeland, throughout a world-wide diaspora, than within the current geographical boundaries of the Republic of Armenia. After the Armenian capital of Yerevan the most populous Armenian city is Moscow. After that comes Los Angeles. As the Armenian people have migrated throughout the world, they have taken with them their church and their liturgy. Every Sunday the Divine Liturgy of the Armenian Church is celebrated in New York, Detroit, Philadelphia, Charlotte, Hollywood (California and Florida!), Dallas; Montreal, Vancouver; Sao Paolo, Buenos Aires, London, Paris, Geneva, Milan, Sophia, Istanbul, St. Petersburg, Samarkand (Uzbekistan), Athens, Aleppo, Beirut, Kuwait City, Baghdad, Teheran, Cairo, Addis Ababa, Calcutta, Sydney, Singapore. And this is just a sampling.

How has the liturgy fared in its global emigration? In October 2001, during the year-long celebrations surrounding the seventeen hundredth anniversary of the proclamation of Christianity as the official religion of Armenia, I was invited to speak to a conference at the University of Southern California co-sponsored by a number of Armenian Church and cultural organizations. The topic assigned to me was:

"The Liturgy of the Armenian Church: Relevance and Reform." Well, this gives us some idea of how successfully the Armenian liturgy has engaged the mostly college-age audience that received me. Evidently these young people do not perceive Schmemann's "something so beautiful, so heavenly, so crucial" in our liturgy.

To put it very simply, our liturgy has become somewhat dysfunctional. By that I mean that the Divine Liturgy is no longer accomplishing what it is supposed to accomplish as effectively as it once did. In specific ways our liturgy is not doing today what it was designed to do, what it claims to do, and what our church fathers said it should do. The vision of the liturgy perceived by the black-shrouded women at St. Hripsimé has become blurred in the eyes of many of our faithful today. Our people are not flocking to the liturgy as we wish they would. Many complain that they do not "understand" the liturgy, or they "don't get anything out of it." Some wonder why the liturgy cannot be modernized, the symbols updated, to become more relevant to their very modern American lives; adapted to engage and respond to a world far removed from the one in which it was conceived. These kinds of remarks from many people suggest that there is a dysfunction in our liturgy, or at least in our apprehension of the liturgy, its nature and purpose. The complex sociological, cultural, and political environment in North America challenges the traditional liturgical life of our churches. The exalted vision of the liturgy I tried to describe is not being communicated to many of our people. I would like to illustrate this assertion by offering three manifestations of this liturgical crisis under the rubrics word, ritual, and mind.

Word: language of the liturgy. There is currently an active and highly controversial movement in the United States to translate the language of the Armenian Church's liturgy into English. Officially, and very recently, by decree of the Supreme Catholicos and Patriarch of All Armenians, the liturgical language was declared to be everywhere and always Classical Armenian. Old Armenian differs decidedly from the eastern and western modern Armenian dialects, somewhat as Latin differs from Italian. Educated native Armenian speakers would recognize some words of a prayer offered in Classical Armenian, but most would have only the vaguest sense of its meaning. The vernacular is increasingly used in the celebration of the sacraments, but not in the Divine Liturgy or the Daily Office.

For many, I am sure, nothing could be more self-evident than the notion that worship should be celebrated in the language of its celebrants.[11] Surely the generations of saints responsible for codifying the words of the Armenian liturgy intended that their prayers and hymns would be comprehended by the people; indeed, that these words, expressing the deepest faith convictions of our people, would have inspirational, transformative — yes, even catechetical — potential. Let us take, for example, this hymn from the Armenian Night Office, composed by the great Armenian hymnographer, theologian, and ecumenist St. Nersess (Shnorhali) the Gracious (†1173):[12]

> Arise, O my glory, arise! And I shall
>   arise in the morning. Alleluia!
> Arise with the vigilant angels, O chil-
>   dren of the supernal Sion. Alleluia!
> Arise, sons of light, in praise of the
>   Father of light. Alleluia! [1Th 5:5]
> Arise, all of you saved by the blood, and
>   give glory to the Savior. Alleluia!
> Arise, new people; sing a new song to
>   Him who makes all things new. Al-
>   leluia! [Ps 96:1]
> Arise, brides in the Spirit, awaiting the
>   coming of the holy Bridegroom. Al-
>   leluia!
> Arise, you, who burn with light, like the
>   wise holy virgins. Alleluia!
> Arise and prepare oil for your lamps
>   with warm tears. Alleluia!

> Arise and sleep not, slumbering like the
>   foolish virgins. Alleluia!
> Arise, let us fall down and worship with
>   tears, saying: Alleluia!
> Arise, why do you sleep? Lord, do not
>   forsake us.
> Arise, Lord, and help us, and we shall
>   give glory to your holy name.
> Now and forever to the Father and to
>   the Son and to the Holy Spirit. Amen.

Is it even remotely conceivable that this sublime meditation, with its elegant ecclesiology, might have been composed and integrated into the liturgy for any reason but to summon God's people in the Armenian Church to acknowledge the gracious dignity of their redemption in Christ, and to live their lives in a manner worthy of this divine vocation? Imagine the impact that this daily hymn would have on worshipers to whom its words are intelligible: extracts and images from sacred Scripture, selected and knitted together according to the deepest theological instinct of the Armenian Church, repeatedly wash over them, awakening faith and devotion; an anamnesis of God's philanthropy, a living Bible study, a catechesis of prayer, the *lex orandi* truly shaping the *lex credendi*.

By contrast, the best-intentioned congregant who has not studied Classical Armenian hears *"Zarteek park eem zarteek yev yes zartyayts aravodoos, alleluia,"* and is left to extract spiritual nourishment from the stirring melody alone, while taking for granted that the repeated refrain, "Alleluia," must be indicative of something worth praising.

Then what prevents the Armenian Church hierarchy from translating the liturgy into the vernacular? Among many other reasons — few of them indisputable — is the socioethnic complexity of the Armenian diaspora today. In short, there is no single vernacular Armenian. As I noted earlier, Classical Armenian evolved into two modern languages — more diverse than dialects — that are spoken in various parts of the world today. Even if the hierarchy were to authorize a more complete inculturation of the liturgy, abandoning modern Armenian for the spoken language of the diocese or even the local parish, the problem would remain. For many Armenian Church parishes in North America English is not the only vernacular. When I was assigned as the visiting pastor of the nascent Armenian community in Charlotte, North Carolina, I found a congregation composed of a smorgasbord of socioethnic subgroups: second and third-generation American-Armenians; settled first-generation American-Armenians from Middle Eastern countries; recent immigrants from Middle Eastern countries; new immigrants from Armenia; and new immigrants from Russia, Azerbaijan, and other former-Soviet republics; and of course non-Armenian spouses and friends. It was a linguistic nightmare. None of my parishioners had anything approaching a working knowledge of Classical Armenian. About half of the American-Armenians knew little or no modern Armenian. The immigrants from Russia and Azerbaijan spoke Russian and halting English; their elders understood some Armenian but had no English, while the children knew no Armenian but had quickly acquired fluent English.

Then there were the more subtle sensitivities. Many of the immigrants — refugees, really — wanted to hear their ancestral language in prayer even if they did not comprehend it. This generation had lost loved ones to ethnic cleansing carried out in Azerbaijan in the late 1980s. They mimicked the sentiments of many of the children of the great Armenian genocide of 1915 perpetrated by Ottoman Turkey. For these people sacrificing the ancestral language is tantamount to betraying the blood of the Armenian martyrs and actually perpetuating the genocide.

Others objected to English in the liturgy not so much ideologically as instinctively. For native Armenian speakers, to address God in the common, spoken idiom rings crude and harsh to the ear. "We must not speak to God in the same language as we speak to the butcher," one man told me. Non-native Armenian speakers can not truly understand such a response.

Still others saw the use of English in the liturgy as a betrayal of orthodoxy. Armenian Protestants are known for praying to, and hymning, God exclusively in the vernacular.

The cultural and linguistic heterogeneity of the Armenian Church's faithful poses a significant challenge to her liturgy's ability to unite, spiritually nourish, and catechize her people, as it consecrates them to the Father.

Ritual: transplanted and rejected. As the vicissitudes of their history have scattered them throughout the world, wherever they have landed Armenians have instinctively reassembled themselves as church. In so doing they have transplanted a very "Eastern" style of worship into the hub of the modern world. Rituals and symbols that arose spontaneously in another world, eloquently evoking there the beliefs and sentiments of the people of that world, have now to speak to the hearts and minds of a community far removed chronologically, geographically, and culturally from the place of their origin. Like a transplanted organ that does not take, there are signs that the Armenian liturgy is being rejected by many Armenians of the new world.

Western Christians should recall the ritual sumptuousness of Eastern liturgy, a seemingly extroverted approach to the worship of God, where gesture and movement inherently co-exist with verbal prayer in a kind of doxological dance. Armenian churches are traditionally pewless for a reason: to facilitate ritual movement and interaction among God's worshipers in the liturgy. Western Christians often come away from Eastern liturgies a bit dizzied, like an introvert who has been overwhelmed by the prolonged company of an extrovert. In like manner cradle Orthodox are puzzled and not a little agitated when invited, in a Protestant or Catholic service, to bow their heads for a few moments of silent, personal reflection following the Gospel reading or the homily.

On the other hand, these distinctions between Eastern and Western attitudes toward worship must not be overdrawn. How, after all, do the categories of East and West relate to a fourth-generation American-Armenian's impression of worship in the Armenian Church of Oakland, California?

Like all ancient Eastern rites, the Armenian Church has preserved a version of the ancient ritual known as the Kiss of Peace. During the preanaphoral rites of the Eucharist, Armenians are bid by the deacons to "Greet one another with a holy kiss" (see Rom 16:16; 1 Cor 16:20; 2 Cor 13:12; 1 Thess 5:26; 1 Peter 5:14). The deacon descends from the elevated bema and offers the ritualized kiss to representatives of the community, who, in turn, pass it along until everyone has received the greeting. The ritual is of course intended to remind Armenians that the sacrifice offered at the altar is futile if they do not first reconcile with one another in their daily lives. The kiss also elegantly and intimately anticipates the love-engendered unity brought about by the Saviour's crucifixion, realized sacramentally in holy communion. In the Armenian Church the kiss of peace is relatively less ritualized than in many other rites where it is practiced. The person offering the kiss bows his head to the left and then to the right of the one receiving the kiss, not quite cheek-to-cheek, while he says, "Christ is revealed among us."

I diverge into these minutiae of ritual for a reason. Some years ago I was invited to celebrate the Divine Liturgy at St. Vartan Armenian Church in Oakland, California. I was not surprised that the church was nearly empty at the beginning of the service. I had long since grown accustomed to my people's less than scrupulous attention to the clock on Sunday mornings (perhaps itself a result of the liturgy's failure to captivate our people). What did surprise me was the sudden influx of a large number of younger people as soon as the Kiss of Peace had been offered. It seemed as though people had been accumulating in the narthex waiting for that moment to enter the sanctuary *en masse.* "They don't like the Kiss of Peace," the pastor explained to me forthrightly after the service. "They feel awkward having their personal space invaded, and embarrassed at not knowing the proper words to say when giving and receiving the kiss." Dysfunctional liturgy, I thought; a beautiful, meaningful, biblical ritual whose significance and import have been distorted owing to a conflict between the liturgy itself and the cultural norms of its celebrants.

Mind: the "modern" need to understand. American-Armenian worshipers in America today bring to the liturgy a mindset quite different from that of the pious old woman who was making her devotional circuit around the exterior walls of the church of St. Hripsimé in Armenia. Our faithful in America are for the most part highly educated, and they want to understand what they are seeing, hearing, and experiencing in the liturgy. They want to bring intellect to worship. They want to get their head around what they are trying to believe. They bring to church all that they have learned and experienced in the technologically advanced, scientific, and secular world we live in. They bring science and logic to theology and liturgy. They want to bring what they see as scientific certainty to their faith. I doubt that the woman at St. Hripsimé worries too much about reconciling her faith with modern science.

The self-conscious desire to bring brains to belief is a sign of modern times. It is the manifestation of a cultural outlook quite different from the one in which our liturgical rites were formed, and were interpreted by the fathers. We, as the result of modern science and our understanding of the universe, not only have a far deeper grasp of the nature of the world that surrounds us than our ancestors did, but we also have far more control over that world and over our own destinies. This is not the place to probe theories of cultural history. What is important is that the modern mentality affects church life as well. People begin to ask unprecedented questions about God, about faith, and about the liturgy.

As a professor of liturgy who is also a priest, I am constantly invited by Armenian church parishes to speak about the meaning of the Divine Liturgy. My hosts invite me in the sincere expectation that I will explain in an hour or so what it all means. Surely there must be someone out there, they assume, who can decipher all of these arcane symbols and movements for them, elucidating all of those strange theological words, and reducing the Divine Liturgy to, say, six easy steps. They hope in vain that I am the one to do this.

Inevitably after my forty-five minute talk I field questions like: Why can't we shorten the liturgy? Why can't we reduce it to its most essential parts? Would the liturgy be "invalid" if we skipped the Trisagion? How can bread and wine become the Body and Blood of Jesus? Can we say "Lord have mercy" once with feeling instead of three times? These are very modern questions. Increasingly, we have to help our people realize that the liturgy is not easy to "understand." It is far from obvious how or why a little bread and wine should become the vehicle for the living Son of God. It is an issue that the fathers and saints of the Armenian church did not "understand" either. They called our Sunday worship service the "Great Mystery." They could believe without "understanding." And this belief was not some vague optimism but a driving faith in a real and living God who, they were convinced, loved them and sustained them.

Alas, many modern, educated Americans are rather uncomfortable in the realm of mystery and faith.

The ability to live peacefully in mystery, what the poet John Keats in the early nineteenth century termed "negative capability," is nothing new to the Christian East.[13] Armenian liturgical texts (as in all Eastern rites) are a virtual festival of apophatic theology, negative descriptions expressing what God is *not*. He is without limits,

infinite, unreachable; he cannot be grasped; he is indescribable, uncontainable, unspeakable, incomprehensible, and more. Hear, for example, this prayer from the Armenian Liturgy of the Word:

O Lord our God, whose power is inscrutable and whose glory incomprehensible, whose mercy is beyond measure and compassion infinite, according to your abundant love of mankind, look down upon this your people and upon this holy temple and make abundant your mercy and your compassion to us and to those who pray with us. For to you is befitting glory, dominion and honor, now and always and unto the ages of ages. Amen.[14]

Does this mean that we are to suppress the questions that come to mind about our faith and worship? Are we to switch off our brains and commit intellectual suicide in order to have a meaningful liturgical experience? By no means; not if we believe that our faith is true. If it is all true, then it will ultimately stand up to any scrutiny we may subject it to. Let us not forget Jesus' promise, "If you continue in my word, you are truly my disciples, and *you will know the truth*, and the truth will make you free" (John 8:31-32); as long as one searches in faith and humility.

I have a sense that deep down we Westernized, "enlightened" Armenian Christians fear that if we peer too deeply into the "mystery" of our faith we will find that the emperor isn't wearing any clothes. I believe that many people fear that if they probe beyond the clichés and allegories, they may find that the liturgy is in fact meaningless; that the Christian faith is, after all, nothing but fictive legends and childish myths; that in the end it is the opiate of the people. They forget the counsel of Scripture:

My son, if you receive my words and treasure up my commandments with you, making your ear attentive to wisdom and inclining your heart to understanding; yes, if you cry out for insight and raise your voice for understanding, if you seek it like silver and search for it as for hidden treasures; then you will understand the fear of the Lord and find the knowledge of God (Prov 2:1-5).

Short of such a determined quest undertaken in faith, however, and in the absence of a new mystagogy that engages, rather than flees from science and honest intellectual inquiry, the Armenian and other Eastern churches in the same predicament will continue to foster in their people at best a superficial faith, compartmentalized and isolated from the rest of reality; or at worst indifference and rejection.

The Armenian Church faces a major and multi-faceted challenge in the years ahead. We must prayerfully discover how fully to engage our people who are, to various degrees, becoming rooted in a culture very different from, and in some cases hostile to, the culture in which our liturgy and Christian vision were forged centuries ago. We will have to convince our people that their Christian tradition, culture, and life represent a viable way for us to live in Christ today. We must reflect seriously on the Christian mission of the Armenian Church in America today. Is our *raison d'être* merely to reach out to, and to serve, Armenians? Will the Armenian Church in America consign itself to the role of spiritual custodian of the steadily assimilating Armenian ethnic ghetto in America? Or does the Armenian Church have a vital message to third-millennium America? A distinctive, truly apostolic Christian witness that is old but new; one, moreover, that is certified by the blood of countless martyrs? Our church will have first to discover for itself, and then to fulfill its God-ordained role in the market-place of North American churches, denominations, and rites. We will have to do this with great care and prudence: engaging and challenging American society and culture, while not betraying our own Christian

identity and distinctive Christian witness. These challenges represent the path ahead, not just for the Armenian Church, but for all ancient Eastern churches that have been transplanted into the United States and other cultures. It is in some ways a frightening path, but an exciting one since, as I am increasingly convinced, it is ordained by divine Providence. I thank you for inviting me to reflect on it with you today.

ENDNOTES

1. For a recent descriptive survey of these rites see Christine Chaillot, "The Ancient Oriental Churches," in *The Oxford History of Christian Worship*, ed. Geoffrey Wainwright and Karen B. Westerfield Tucker (New York: Oxford University Press, 2006), 131-69.

2. See Abraham Terian, *Patriotism and Piety in Armenian Christianity: The Early Panegyrics on Saint Gregory*. AVANT: Treasures of the Armenian Christian Tradition 2 (Crestwood, N.Y.: St. Vladimir's Seminary Press and St. Nersess Armenian Seminary, 2005); ibid., "Surpassing the Biblical Worthies: An Early Motif in Armenian Religious Literature," *St. Nersess Theological Review* 1 (July 1996), 117-44. Robert W. Thomson, ed., *Elishe: History of Vardan and the Armenian War* (Cambridge, Mass.: Harvard University Press, 1982), 9-21.

3. The best presentation of the overall history and features of the Armenian Rite is Robert F. Taft, S.J., "The Armenian Liturgy: Its Origins and Characteristics," in *Treasures in Heaven: Armenian Art, Religion and Society, Papers delivered at the Pierpont Morgan Library at a Symposium organized by Thomas F. Mathews and Roger S. Wieck 21-22 May 1994* (New York: The Pierpont Morgan Library, 1998), 13-30.

4. For an historical, comparative study of the Daily Offices of the Armenian Church with complete bibliography see my *The Commentary on the Daily Office of the Armenian Church by Bishop Step'anos Siwnec'i (c. 685-735): Edition of the Long and Short Recensions with Liturgical Analysis*. Orientalia Christiana Analecta 270. (Rome: Pontificio Istituto Orientale, 2004).

5. Robert F. Taft, S.J., *Beyond East and West: Problems in Liturgical Understanding,* 2d rev. and enlarged edition (Rome: Edizioni Orientalia Christiana, 1997), 304.

6. "Liturgy" in *Westminster Dictionary of Theological Terms,* ed. Donald K. McKim (Louisville: Westminster John Knox Press, 1996), 128.

7. For further reflections on these ideas see Robert F. Taft, S.J., "Toward a Theology of the Liturgy of the Hours," in his *The Liturgy of the Hours in East and West: The Origins of the Divine Office and Its Meaning for Today* (Collegeville: The Liturgical Press, 1986), 331-65.

8. Alexander Schmemann, *Liturgy and Life: Christian Development through Liturgical Experience* (New York: Orthodox Church in America, 1983), 74.

9. The story of the conversion of the Armenian king and of the Armenian people to Christianity is recounted in the fifth-century *History of the Armenians* ascribed to a certain Agat'angełos. For an English translation see R. W. Thomson, *Agathangelos: History of the Armenians* (Albany: State University of New York, 1976).

10. Nina G. Garsoïan, "The History of Armenia," in *Treasures in Heaven: Armenian Illuminated Manuscripts,* ed. Thomas F. Mathews and Roger S. Wieck (New York: The Pierpont Morgan Library and Princeton University Press, 1994), 3-23, presents a convenient summary of Armenian history by one of its foremost living scholars.

11. Here I do not intend "celebrants" in a clerical sense, but in the ecclesial sense of all of God's people gathered for the liturgy as concelebrants of the Eucharist, and, by extension, of the church's entire liturgical life.

12. My translation of *Žamagirkʻ ateni [Book of Hours]*, (Jerusalem: Sts. James Press, 1915), 187. I am not aware of any previous published translations of this hymn.

13. For a thought-provoking reflection, see Kathleen Norris, "Exile, Homeland and Negative Capability," in her *The Cloister Walk* (New York: Riverhead Books, 1996), 53-70.

14. Daniel Findikyan, ed., *The Divine Liturgy of the Armenian Church with Modern Armenian and English Translations, Transliteration, Musical Notation, Introduction and Notes* (New York: St. Vartan Press, 1999), 12

Michael Daniel Findikyan is an ordained priest of the Armenian Orthodox Church and professor of liturgical studies at St. Nersess Armenian Seminary, New Rochelle, New York. Following completion of the M.Div. from St. Vladimir's Orthodox Theological Seminary, Crestwood, New York, and St. Nersess Armenian Seminary, as well as the M.A. in musicology from City University of New York, he studied with Robert Taft, S.J., at the Pontifical Oriental Institute in Rome, earning a doctoral degree in liturgical studies in 1997. He has written numerous studies on the liturgies of the Christian East including a monograph on the historical development of the Armenian Daily Office. He is a recurring visiting professor at the University of Notre Dame.

Inculturation: The Bread and Wine at the Eucharist

PHILLIP TOVEY

On Sunday mornings when I preside at the Eucharist I keep an eye out for one of the people in the congregation. If she is there I put a square wafer in the ciborium at the preparation of the table. She has celiac disease, and under the guise of pastoral sensitivity it has become the norm to add the special wafer. I do not even think about the wine, which is usually fortified to stop it going bad.

Questions of inculturation are complex because we are so immersed in our own culture that we often cannot see the wood for the trees. Culture is like that: in it we live and move and have our being. Finding that something does not quite fit our expectations becomes a critical incident for us.[1] It is often easier to see what is being done wrong than to reflect upon our own actions; motes and beams come to mind.

I want to look at the material for the Eucharist, bread and wine, partially because this is the key act of worship of Christians, partially because it has been an issue for me in my ministry, and partially because it is causing some concern in Anglican circles at present. Thus it represents for me work in progress, a development of the comments in my earlier work.[2]

Church of England Rubrics and Canons

The Church of England uses bread and wine. The 1604 canons talked of the churchwardens providing "fine white bread" and "good and wholesome wine" (Canon 20). The 1662 *Book of Common Prayer* of the Church of England says that to avoid dissention or superstition it shall "suffice that the Bread such as is usual to be eaten: but the best and purest Wheat Bread that conveniently may be gotten." This followed the change in 1552; in 1549 the directions were that the bread be "unleavened and round, as it was before, but without all manner of print,

and something more larger and thicker than it was, so that it may be aptly divided in divers pieces" (spelling modernized). Elizabeth tried to insist on unleavened bread in 1559 but this met with much opposition and was unenforceable. Anglicans have from time to time argued for or against wafers and bread.

The canons of the Church of England now say: "The bread, whether leavened or unleavened, shall be of the best and purest wheat flower that conveniently may be gotten, and the wine the fermented juice of the grape, good and wholesome."[3] The present canon clearly reflects a number of historical discussions:

• firstly, conceding the push of the catholic revival to use unleavened bread; achieving what Elizabeth was unable to do;

• secondly, fending off the push of the Free Churches to use grape juice instead of wine.

This may seem to draw the issue to a close but there is one context where more rules apply. Local Ecumenical Partnerships (LEPs) are designated areas of ecumenical cooperation where more than one denomination work together. I worked in one on a new housing estate where five denominations shared one building. There was a Roman Catholic congregation, a congregation of Brethren, and a "Shared Congregation" of Anglicans, Methodists, and Reformed, where I was the Anglican priest and I shared in ministry to the congregation with a Reformed minister. Anglicans have quite complex rules for such situations, including one on the eucharistic elements: "Where a priest of the Church of England is presiding at a service of Holy Communion according to the rite of another Church…and there are conscientious objections from members of other Churches to alcoholic wine, at least real grape juice should be used, and fermented wine from which the alcohol has been removed is to be preferred."[4] This has been a contentious issue in some LEPs, and this tries to provide a sliding scale of priorities:

- real wine;
- if there is objection, dealcoholized wine, or
- grape juice.

This scale brings me to another experience in my ministry, in the Church of Uganda.

Church of Uganda. From 1983–1985 I was the chaplain of Archbishop Janani Luwum Theological College in Northern Uganda. This was the post-Amin period, and the economy was devastated. It was clear that Uganda was once a prosperous country, but all that had now disappeared, ravaged by war. Part of my job was to purchase elements for the chapel. Bread was available, but it was a luxury item, and from a Ugandan perspective not a staple "daily bread" but something produced for an honored guest. A further problem with bread was that in the tropical climate it did not last very long. The Roman Catholic Church had plenty of wafers, which were sold at a reasonable price, and this was what we used in chapel. They were easy to get and lasted in the climate. On the few occasions when this was not possible biscuits were used.

Wine however was a big problem. Most of the time it was not available. Grapes do not grow in Uganda, and there is no tradition of drinking wine in the local culture. The only things in the shops were whiskey and ribena (concentrated blackcurrant juice). Wine when available was super-expensive—e.g., one bottle of wine cost the equivalent of three months' collections in my local church. Most of the time we used ribena, but sometimes whiskey. Thus I was left with a different sliding scale to the Church of England. Do I select:

- whiskey, alcoholic, but pale in color, or
- ribena, non-alcoholic, but red in color?

Neither of them is related to the grape. History in Uganda showed that this was a problem for the church during most of its existence.

The peoples of Uganda do not grow grapes or wheat. Neither of these crops is native to the country, bananas being the staple in the south and millet in the north. These staples are eaten with a variety of vegetables. It is technically possible to grow both crops—you can, after all, ski on the equator in Uganda—but the reality is that they have to be imported.

The first missionaries walked across what is now Tanzania and were then paddled across Lake Victoria. They had all their provisions carried for them. In 1877 CMS missionaries arrived in Buganda. In 1895 Bishop Tucker arrived.[5] He soon realized that the provision of communion wine was an issue. By January 1896 he had "provisionally" sanctioned the use of native wine from the juice of bananas. It would appear that this continued off and on until the coming of the railway, and thus a reliable supply route. This was taken into account again in the Amin years, and with the economic collapse of the country banana wine was used by the church alongside other materials. Indeed, the Church of Uganda has a canon that says: "In absence of grape wine well-boiled banana juice wine or pineapple or passion fruit wine may be used, in consultation with the bishop" (2.13.3). Here is another sliding scale: if no grape wine, use fruit wines from local fruits.

International Anglican Agreement. A further dimension to the whole issue is the international statements that Anglicans have made. The Lambeth conference of 1888 resolved that one basis for reunion was "The Supper of the Lord —ministered with unfailing use of Christ's words of institution, and of the elements ordained by Him." This became a part of the Lambeth Quadrilateral, which gained sufficient authority for the Episcopal Church to include it in "Historical Documents" of *The Book of Common Prayer* (1979). It begs the question of the elements ordained by Christ, which we will come to later.

While the international Lambeth conferences kept agreeing on bread and wine as

Christ instituted, we have already seen that local variations had begun to occur. Eventually this was acknowledged. The 1989 Inter Anglican Liturgical Consultation raised some questions: "Sacramental elements: here there are special problems, needing more work. Should wafer bread be as dominant as it needs to be—even to the point of being imported? Should local staple food and drink supervene? How far can variations be allowed?"[6]

The questions were raised but no answers were forthcoming. This was repeated in the Kanamai Statement of 1993, a regional meeting of African Anglicans: "We wish to encourage local people to produce the eucharistic bread and to ask the provinces to consider whether they should permit the use of local staple foods and drinks for the eucharistic elements, also carefully considering this alongside the biblical tradition."[7] The 1995 Dublin Report was more cautious. Commenting directly on the above statement this Conference said: "This should be seen as a decision to be considered at the Provincial level rather than by individual congregations. Because the use of a different eucharistic species has implications for the worldwide Anglican Communion, before implementing such a decision Provinces are encouraged to consult the worldwide Communion through such bodies as the IALC, The Anglican Consultative Council, and the Lambeth Conference."[8]

A preliminary report on this[9] shows much more variation than had been realized, and so the IALC was asked in 2002 to do further work on the eucharistic elements by ACC 12 which said that it "awaits a survey by the Inter Anglican Liturgical Consultation of practice in relation to the elements of Holy Communion in the churches of the Anglican Communion, and of the reasons given for any departure from dominical command" (resolution 16.1). The last phrase, "departure from dominical command," sounds rather heavy but still begs the question. This is work in progress and the potential tensions are hinted at in the text.

Eucharistic Symbols

You may by now be thinking that this is a tiresome discussion. One colleague in a group debate said that all these machinations were irrelevant; the Eucharist is about inclusion, and so you had to be pragmatic concerning the elements. Other people might say that it is only a symbol, and this discussion sounds like angels on pinheads. Such statements have implicit approaches to eucharistic symbols and do not necessarily escape the issues. So some comments about symbolism may illuminate the discussion.

Many who study symbolism would want to say that they are highly important in conveying cultural meaning. Symbols condense the values and thoughts of a culture, and they are polysemic, they have more than one meaning. So they are more than "only a symbol." To some students of symbols this is almost an oxymoron. Victor Turner,[10] a Christian anthropologist, talked of the two poles of a symbol:

- one around the ideology,
- and one around the physical elements.

The two are connected. This is helpful as it illumines some of the issues around what to use for wine. Wine gathers around it a number of meanings:

- festal drink,
- Blood of Christ,
- Last Supper,
- Passover connection,
- eschatological judgment,
- gladdening the heart,
- shared cup.

To these might be added

- family food,
- local produce,

particularly where you grow your own. However in other parts of the world, where wine is not a staple or a local product, other meanings may attach to the symbol:

- luxury item,
- foreign drink,

• prohibited drink to neighbors (in Islamic regions),

   • temptation to drunkenness.

Some of these meanings are supplied by the elements, others by the biblical tradition, and others by the local culture. These meanings may at time conflict with one another, and people's arguments may draw on a number of these meanings at any one time. If some stress fidelity to what Jesus used at the Last Supper, clearly others, including my colleague, stress inclusion from the shared cup. Turner's contribution to this debate is to show that these complex webs of meanings underlie our discourse on such matters. We implicitly rank these various meanings, and undertake debate based on our own rankings. This can even influence our use of the Bible.

Biblical traditions. Cyprian's letter to Caecilius (*Ep.* 62),[11] written in 253, argues that we must do what Jesus did, and that deviation from this tradition is erroneous. This led to a debate centering on the narratives of institution in the Scriptures. More recent studies have widened the scope of the discussion by looking at Jesus' meal traditions, some of which have eucharistic resonances, for example in the story of the disciples on the road to Emmaus. While *artos* is the word used for bread in this narrative, we find that in John (6:9) the feeding of the five thousand is with barley bread. Even more interestingly, Luke, mentioning the feast of unleavened bread (22:1), uses the word for unleavened bread, *azumos*, while in his last supper narrative (22:19) he uses *artos*. Luke contains the "cup, bread, cup" order; his is the only narrative with two cups (or it does if you follow the longer text; otherwise it has the "cup, bread" order, following the shorter version of the text, which omits verses 19b-20).

Paul Bradshaw uses this and much other evidence to suggest that there was diversity of practice both in the New Testament and the early church.[12] This includes the normal bread and cup, the agape with Eucharist, the cup bread tradition, and a bread and water tradition. Indeed, some of these variations in the text became the focus of a dispute between the Eastern and Western churches, with the East using leavened bread, arguing that *artos* is not *azumos*, and the West arguing that the Last Supper was a Passover meal and therefore must have used unleavened bread.[13]

Meanwhile, from a different ideological perspective there are still those today who argue for different meanings of the word "wine" in the Bible.[14] Here the case is that the prohibitions on drunkenness and unethical use of wine require a distinction between grape juice and alcoholic wine. The argument is that grape juice, either fresh or boiled, was used at Jewish festivals, not fermented wine. This means that Jesus would not have used fermented wine at the Last Supper, and neither should we. This comes in part from the temperance tradition, but the case is also raised from other traditions. Some Muslims have argued that the prophet Jesus would not have used wine, as holy men do not drink alcohol.[15] Clearly the picture is complex, and our ideological starting point, in this case support of the temperance movement (or Islam), is one factor in the hermeneutics of exegetics and historical study. Some in this camp note approvingly of the use of grapes or raisins in Oriental Churches as supporting their arguments, but dimensions to the practice of these churches widen the issues.

I was watching the deacon make the eucharistic bread in a Syrian Orthodox church in Kerala, South India. He took some dough from a tin, added more flour and water, and made small rolls, while putting some of the dough back. The rolls were then pressed onto a mold to produce a round cake about two inches in diameter. This was cooked over the censer, which incidentally had charcoal from the husks of surrounding coconut trees. The cakes were then used in the Eucharist. The key element in this process is the dough. A piece is always kept and used for the next Eucharist. It was explained to me that this was the "holy leaven," dough going back to the bread that Jesus used at the Last Supper. These traditions are also found in the Coptic Church, Ethiopian Orthodox Church, and the Church of the East.[16] I do not buy the strict historical accuracy of this narrative, but it shows a different cultural agenda in the debate concerning the correct elements for the Eucharist. Here the important link is the physical connection between this Eucharist and Jesus in the dough.

The Roman Catholic Approach

Controversy over the elements, and particularly the bread in relation to celiac disease, is not confined to Anglicanism. This has caused a number of discussions in the Roman Catholic Church. The 1983 *Code of Canon Law*[17] states:

> Can. 924 §1. The most holy eucharistic sacrifice must be offered with bread and with wine in which a little water must be mixed. §2. The bread must be only wheat and recently made so that there is no danger of spoiling. §3. The wine must be natural from the fruit of the vine and not spoiled. Can. 926. According to the ancient tradition of the Latin Church, the priest is to use unleavened bread in the eucharistic celebration whenever he offers it.

The bread therefore must be wheat bread and unleavened "according to ancient tradition." The *Catechism of the Catholic Church*[18] explains:

> 1412 The essential signs of the Eucharistic sacrament are wheat bread and grape wine, on which the blessing of the Holy Spirit is invoked and the priest pronounces the words of consecration spoken by Jesus during the Last Supper: "This is my body which will be given up for you. ... This is the cup of my blood ..."

The 1975 *General Instruction of the Roman Missal*[19] adds some comments about the bread:

> 281. Following the example of Christ, the Church has always used bread and wine with water to celebrate the Lord's Supper. 282. According to the tradition of the entire Church, the bread must be made from wheat; according to the tradition of the Latin Church, it must be unleavened. 283. The nature of the sign demands that the material for the eucharistic celebration truly have the appearance of food. Accordingly, even though unleavened and baked in the traditional shape, the eucharistic bread should be made in such a way that in a Mass with a congregation the priest is able actually to break the host into parts and distribute them to at least some of the faithful. (When, however, the number of communicants is large or other pastoral needs require it, small hosts are in no way ruled out.) The action of the breaking of the bread, the simple term for the eucharist in apostolic times, will more clearly bring out the force and meaning of the sign of the unity of all in the one bread and of their charity, since the one bread is being distributed among the members of one family. 284. The wine for the eucharist must be from the fruit of the vine (see Lk 22:18), natural, and pure, that is not mixed with any foreign substance.

This might seem to rule out any use of alternative elements. However, there is a certain amount of "reading in" to say that the Church has always used bread and wine mixed with water. Bradshaw (op. cit.) would argue that there were orthodox Christian groups using only water. The Instruction that the bread should have appearance of food also raises questions about wafers. Do they really look like food? Notice too that "the tradition of the Latin Church" is an interesting cultural linguistic self-designation.

This led to a rather definite directive from the then Cardinal Ratzinger, who in 1994 argued in relation to Celiac disease:

IB 1) Special hosts "*quibus glutinum ablatum est*" [that are gluten-free] are invalid matter for the celebration of the Eucharist.

2) Low-gluten hosts are valid matter, provided that they contain the amount of gluten sufficient to obtain the confection of bread, that there is no addition of foreign materials and that the procedure for making such hosts is not such as to alter the nature of the substance of the bread.

He also commented on the wine in the context of alcoholic priests:

II. B… the permission to use *mustum* can be granted by ordinaries to priests affected by alcoholism or other conditions which prevent the ingestion of even the smallest quantity of alcohol, after presentation of a medical certificate.

C. By "mustum" is understood fresh juice from grapes or juice preserved by suspending its fermentation (by means of freezing or other methods which do not alter its nature).

He thus concludes:

III. D. Given the centrality of the celebration of the Eucharist in the life of the priest, candidates for the priesthood who are affected by celiac disease or suffer from alcoholism or similar conditions may not be admitted to holy orders.[20]

This all follows very logically from the definitions; it is a law-based approach that has defined bread and wine and which then regulates permitted variations from that essentialist definition, i.e. low-gluten bread (but not gluten free), and mustum, preserved grape juice, for the wine. Clearly my own practice does not follow the Roman Catholic approach.

Processes of Inculturation

There are therefore a variety of approaches to the "correct" bread and wine. The definitive statements of the Vatican have not stopped Catholics in places such as Africa, who are arguing for a change in the law, from pointing out that bread and wine are elements of a particular mediterranean culture.[21] A number of different processes have been suggested for inculturation:

- adaptation;
- creative assimilation;
- pastoral sensitivity;
- dynamic equivalence.

Adaptation is the term used by the fathers of the Second Vatican Council in *Sacrosanctum Concilium*.[22] Examples of adaptation are using the vernacular, new musical traditions, preferring oil lamps to candles.

Creative assimilation is the bringing in of something from a culture to the liturgy. The Lutheran *Nairobi Statement* calls it "adding pertinent components of local culture to the liturgical ordo in order to enrich its core" (3.4).[23] Clear examples of this are the development of secondary symbolism at baptism and the incorporation of vows into a marriage liturgy. Nowadays people usually think that vows are a central part of marriage, but it is clear that this is a later tradition, and that vows in marriage rites were an introduction in the West at the turn of the first millennium. Vows are still not a part of Eastern marriage rites.

Pastoral sensitivity drives me to use gluten-free wafers, and grape juice for alcoholics. For me the issue is not legislating for the clergy but consideration of the position of people within the eucharistic community.

Almost unnoticed, many of us are using *dynamic equivalence*. The Lutheran *Narobi Statement* is again clear: "It involves re-expressing components of Christian worship with something from a local culture that has an equal meaning, value and function … it involves … enabling the meanings and actions of worship to be 'encoded' and re-expressed in the language of local culture" (3.2). I want to suggest that some of us do that Sunday by Sunday without even noticing.

In my local church we use wafers and wine. The wine is fortified to preserve it. This is very common in Anglican churches. Other places use leavened bread, often purchased from a local shop. The conscious element in the choice is churchmanship—wafers vs. "real bread"—and denominational identity—wine, not grape juice. A secondary reflection on the material used shows that wafers are hard to conceive as bread at all. Unleavened bread is now available in the shops, not least to be eaten with curry and large amounts of beer. Wafers bear little resemblance to this. What we do know is that at the last supper Jesus did not use round quasi-bread, nor did he use fortified wine. We do not even know that he mixed wine with water—even that is a later tradition. What we have unconsciously done is an adaptation by a process of dynamic equivalence, using what approximates and holds the equivalent meaning of bread and wine. If we can recognize that this is what we do, then perhaps we can begin to consider the position of others who live in contexts where bread and wine are not available.

Methodological considerations. A further problem that underlies the discussion is a problem of definition. When is something an adaptation, and is this the same as inculturation? Should the whole issue be incorporated into the debate about contextualization? It is a question of drawing your boxes, defining your categories. Maybe inculturation is the way liturgical studies have referred to issues having to do with cultural particularity, which other branches of theology have debated under the category of contextualization. A common language has yet to be developed.

Even within the scope of this article different methodological approaches to issues of the eucharistic species can be seen. These can be summarized as follows:

• Ideological: Jesus cannot have used wine because he was a good Muslim (Abdullah) or a holy person (Ostling). From my perspective a priori reasoning is being used in these arguments, in the reading of texts.

• Juridical: this can be seen in the approach of some Roman Catholics. From a definition of bread logical consequences are developed. The danger I see here is the increasing *reductio ad absurdum* over how much gluten can be left out before it ceases to be bread.

• Symbolical: this can be seen in the Lutheran *Nairobi Statement* and its comments on dynamic equivalence. A problem would seem to be that you can never replace something with something else of equal meaning, and you are always left with a judgment whether the fit is close enough. The situation is complex, with competing methodologies, hence the variety of approaches in the different churches. So what does the liturgical practitioner do on Sunday?

Back to my local church. I began this discussion in my local church with the gluten-free wafer. There never was much of a conscious decision about using this wafer; indeed it was something I inherited, and I continued the tradition. It was only when the question was raised in an inter-Anglican context that I began to question what had happened. I suspect that inculturation by dynamic equivalence, or assimilation, is very much like that. It happens almost without our noticing it. As to the Roman Catholic approach, I am not sure that they will escape this either. Indeed, the adoption of wafers in the West may well be "a more radical adaptation" for all sorts of reasons that are now forgotten. Jesus took bread and a cup and gave thanks. Christians today have to work out how this should be done in their own cultural context. They do not all agree.

ENDNOTES

1. See C. Chadwick and P. Tovey, *Growing in Ministry: Using Critical Incident Analysis.* Grove Pastoral Series

(Cambridge: Grove Books, 2000), 84.

2. P. Tovey, *Inculturation of Christian Worship* (Basingstoke: Ashgate, 2004).

3. *The Canons of the Curch of England*, 6th ed. (London: CHP, 2000), B17.2.

4. General Synod of the Church of England, *Ecumenical Relations Canons B 43 and B 44: Code of Practice* (London: General Synod, 1987), 21.

5. A. P. Shepherd, *Tucker of Uganda: Artist and Apostle* (London: SCM, 1929).

6. D. R. Holeton, ed., *Liturgical Inculturation in the Anglican Communion*. JLS 15 (Bramcote: Grove Books, 1990), 11.

7. D. Gitari, ed., *Liturgical Inculturation in Africa: The Kanamai Statement "African Culture and Anglican Liturgy."* JLS 28 (Nottingham: Grove Books, 1994), 41.

8. J. M. Rosental and N. Currie, *Being Anglican in the Third Millennium* (Harrisburg: Morehouse, 1977), 325.

9. P. Gibson, *International Anglican Liturgical Consultations: Minutes from Berkeley 2001*, http://www.anglicancommunion.org/documents/liturgy/ialc2001minutes.html#navmap, (accessed 03/02), 2001.

10. See V. Turner and E. Turner, *Image and Pilgrimage in Christian Culture* (Oxford: Blackwell, 1978).

11. Cyprian, "To Caecilius, on the Sacrament and the Cup of the Lord," trans. Ernest Wallis, in *The Ante-Nicene Fathers*, ed. A. Roberts and J. Donaldson (Grand Rapids: Eerdmans, 1957), 5:358-64.

12. See P. Bradshaw, *Eucharistic Origins* (London: SPCK, 2004).

13. See B. D. Woolley, *The Bread of the Eucharist* (London: Mowbrays, 1913).

14. R. Ostling, *Should Wine, Grape Juice or Water Be Consumed at Communion?* http://www.news-star.com/stories/060102/rel_1.shtml (accessed 10/04), 2002.

15. O. Abdullah, "If Jesus was Muslim as Muslims claim, then why did he convert water into wine in one case, and said that wine is his blood in another since wine and alcohol are prohibited in Islam?" http://www.answering-christianity.com/que18.htm (accessed, 10/04), n.d.

16. See E. S. Drower, *Water into Wine* (London: John Murray, 1956).

17. http://www.vatic an.va/archive/ENG1104/__P3A.HTM (accessed 10/04).

18. http://www.vatican.va/archive/catechism/p2s2c1a3.htm#VII (accessed 10/04).

19. http://www.ewtn.com/library/CURIA/GIRM.HTM#2 (accessed 10/04).

20. Congregation for the Doctrine of the Faith, *Norms for Use of Low-gluten Bread and Mustum*, http://www.adoremus.org/CDF_Lowgluten-mustum94.html (accessed 10/04), 1994.

21. See E. E. Uzukwu, "Food and Drink in Africa and the Christian Eucharist," *AFER* 72 (1980): 370-85; E. A. Ruch, "Food and Drink in the Eucharist [a response to Uzukwu]," *AFER* 73, (1981): 179-81.

22. http://www.vatican.va/archive/hist_councils/ii_vatican_council/documents/vat-ii_const_19631204_sacrosanctum-concilium_en.html (accessed 06/04), 1963.

23. The Lutheran World Federation, *Nairobi Statement*, http://www.worship.ca/docs/lwf_ns.html (accessed 06/04), 1996.

Dr. Phillip Tovey is an Anglican priest, director of reader training for the Diocese of Oxford, and liturgy lecturer at Ripon College, Cuddesdon. He is also program director for a Masters in Ministry. He has degrees from the University of London, University of Nottingham, and Oxford Brookes University. He ministered for twelve years in parishes in the Diocese of Oxford, and worked for two years for the Diocese of Northern Uganda. He has published numerous articles and monographs on liturgy and worship. His last book was Inculturation of Christian Worship, *published by Ashgate.*

The Making of the Church of Ireland *Book of Common Prayer* 2004

HAROLD MILLER

In the 2004 Church of Ireland *Book of Common Prayer* the Preface describes the work of compilation in the following words:

• We sought to unify the worship of God's people, while allowing reasonable scope for diversity within the essential unity of the Church's prayer.

• We were determined to produce a book which would have equal capacity to enrich private as well as corporate devotion.

• We desired that this book, like previous editions of it, should properly articulate and embody the Church's faith.

• We hoped that the book would strengthen our bonds of unity with sister churches who share our approach to common prayer, and we were therefore fully attentive to the reports of successive meetings of the International Anglican Liturgical Consultation.

These sentences capture, in a brief and simple form, some of the key elements that have been distinguishing features of Irish Anglican worship and ethos over the centuries, and that are of great importance to our self-understanding in the Church of Ireland. To put them in other words: the commonality of prayer; the relationship between public and private worship; *lex orandi, lex credendi*; and a sense of worldwide catholicity. In this lecture, I will take these four areas one by one, and use them as windows into the making of the new Church of Ireland *Book of Common Prayer*.

Unity in Diversity: The Commonality of Prayer

We sought to unify the worship of God's people, while allowing reasonable scope for diversity within the essential unity of the Church's prayer.

A quick review of prayer books in the Anglican Communion would show many liturgical volumes that are more flexible, more incultur-ated, more imaginative, and more "on the edge" theologically than the liturgies of the Church of Ireland. For example, apart from a list of Celtic saints and their dates, and one or two Irish propers, some Irish hymns in the hymnal, and the fact that there is an Irish edition of the new BCP, there are very few signs of Celtic spirituality in the formal worship books of the Church of Ireland. While characteristics such as flexibility, inculturation, and imagination are not in any sense absent from the 2004 *Book of Common Prayer*, the book is nevertheless characterized above all else by a desire for unity in the worship of God's people—something greatly treasured in the Church of Ireland, not least because of our other political, cultural, and theological divisions on the island of Ireland. This desire is, therefore, part of our own inculturation in a varied and sometimes divided community. The theme song of the 1878 Preface to the *Book of Common Prayer* is very much part of the psyche of the Church of Ireland when it states: "What is imperfect with peace is often better than what is otherwise more excellent without it."

It might not immediately be noticed by those outside Ireland that the Church of Ireland functions in two different political jurisdictions. The vast majority of members of the Church of Ireland are in Northern Ireland, which is part of the United Kingdom; they generally see their primary identity as being British, and are Unionist by political persuasion. However, the church is administratively centered in Dublin, in the Republic of Ireland, where most of our ordinands are trained, and where our General Synod has normally been held. Our members in the Republic would almost all be Nationalist in political persuasion. And many of our dioceses straddle the border. It is in this context that the *Book of Common Prayer* needs to have an intentionally unifying role.

To help you understand this I will take you back for a moment to the experience of the Church of Ireland when the 1984 *Alternative Prayer Book* was introduced. This made the Church of Ireland, for the first time, a church of two books. The model was, of course, the Church of England, with its 1980 *Alternative Service Book* alongside the 1662 *Book of Common Prayer*. (Interestingly, you will notice that both the 1984 APB and the 2004 BCP were published, in each case, precisely four years after the Church of England produced their key liturgical works, the *Alternative Service Book* and *Common Worship*. This is, I think, a symbol of an instinctive dependence of the Church of Ireland on England in liturgical revision, which has sometimes displayed itself in the past as fearfulness that we, as a small church, might do the wrong thing! In the revisions of services in the 1980s and 1990s, the resultant Church of Ireland liturgies were often very similar to those of the Church of England, but usually with less variety, less novelty, and less theological "risk.")

However, even with this carefulness, when the APB was introduced in 1984 it was not by any means universally welcomed. For many parishes—those which had used the experimental "booklets" produced between 1967 and 1984—the transition was smooth, and the desire to have a book again for Sunday worship was great. However, many of the new booklets were firmly resisted in more conservative parishes, and sections of the Orange Order condemned some of the new liturgies (especially the eucharistic liturgies) as Romish. This meant that they were firmly resisted by Select Vestries (who had no actual constitutional role in deciding forms of worship, but had great "moral" power in the parishes) in large sections especially of rural Ulster. Stories are still told of clergy who attempted to introduce the APB only to have Select Vestries refuse to pay for it, and people refuse to take the book, or to worship when it was being used. The 1926 *Book of Common Prayer* then became the symbol of all things "protestant" in these areas,

and was held on to by some for grim death.

In other parts of the country, for example in the Diocese of Cork where I ministered for many years, the old *Book of Common Prayer* (1926) services were rarely used after 1984, and the APB became ubiquitous.

Churches therefore became either "BCP" parishes or "APB" parishes, and some, trying to steer a middle course with an emphasis on the word "Alternative" in the APB, tried to ride two horses at the same time. This led to a great deal of confusion about whether this was an "And also with you" Sunday or a "And with thy spirit" Sunday!

Alongside this, as the 1990s progressed, it became clear that several aspects of the revised services were wearing thin quite quickly. There was the obvious question of non-inclusive language in relation to people—oddly more pervasive in the "contemporary" liturgies—and a list of suitable amendments had to be issued by the Liturgical Advisory Committee to make the language more inclusive. Then there was the lectionary, which was thematic and based on the work of the Joint Liturgical Group in Britain. Unfortunately the APB had overly highlighted the theme of each Sunday by placing it as a heading to the readings. The themes, in use since the early seventies, were becoming tired and worn and were providing a very limited diet, and indeed interpretation, of scripture. Also, the JLG lectionary, with its "quirky" beginning of the Christian year on the "Ninth Sunday before Christmas," was not proving popular. Since the lectionary readings, printed in full as they were, took up about half the pages in the APB, the introduction of the *Revised Common Lectionary* into the Church of Ireland in 1996 made the APB, in effect, a "dead duck" as a book for the future. These and other issues (for example the lack of poetry in much of the liturgical writing of the seventies, and the lack of flexibility in many of the services) meant that things were straining at the edges; and (although I remember a boo or two when I made a speech suggesting this to the General Synod) there was a general recognition that changes would have to take place in the more contemporary forms of worship.

In 1995 the Liturgical Advisory Committee, recognizing these emerging issues, and also noting that both of the present prayer books were rapidly going out of print, made the following observation in its report to the General Synod:

> With the promised publication of a new edition of the hymnbook in 2000 . . . [Like ECUSA, the Church of Ireland has an official hymnbook, and the fifth edition of the *ChurchHymnal* was being complied at thetime]…, the LAC believes that the time has come for a "Sunday Services Book" to complement the new hymnbook. It envisages such a book as a unifying book (there's the theme again), containing the materials required for normal congregational worship drawn from the *Book of Common Prayer* [i.e., of 1926] and alternative services in the *Alternative Prayer Book.*

It then listed the possible contents of such a Sunday Services Book, which are relatively obvious.

One of the ways the Church of Ireland seeks to achieve unity and general agreement in its worship is by filtering it through a thoroughgoing and sometimes tedious two-year synodical process. (The General Synod meets annually.) It is vital at any stage to determine the mood of the synod, to gain its confidence, and to respond to its concerns. In this case the Synod of 1995 left the liturgical committee with an interesting quandary. It was clear from the voting that the "Sunday Services Book" way forward had not received the requisite two-thirds majority which a liturgical resolution requires in both houses. Two-thirds had not been achieved in the lay vote. However, on the last day of the Synod a new resolution was placed before the whole synod in an attempt to rescue the situation "encouraging

the Liturgical Advisory Committee to proceed in producing a future book along the lines outlined…" As the committee reflected on this over the succeeding year, it decided to present what was in fact a much more radical model. Instead of a Sunday services book that would have made three Church of Ireland worship books (BCP, *Alternative Occasional Services*, and the new publication), the General Synod was presented with a possible proposal for a thorough revision of the *Book of Common Prayer* itself, "such revision to include services in traditional language and also in contemporary language and liturgical style."

This was a major change because, although there had been revisions of the *Book of Common Prayer* over the previous 125 years, most of these, even the major ones in 1878 and 1926, were essentially tinkering with the text. Now there was the possibility of the most major transformation of the BCP in its 450 years of history. The final go-ahead was given in 1998, and a timetable provided, leading to the launching of the 2004 *Book of Common Prayer* six years later at a General Synod service at which Archbishop Rowan Williams preached. This was the first General Synod ever to be held in the primatial city of Armagh.

There is no doubt in my mind that the 2004 *Book of Common Prayer* is proving to be a unifying book. From Advent Sunday 2005 it has become the only legal prayer book of the Church of Ireland; its sales have been absolutely enormous; it has been made available in electronic form in a special Irish version of *Visual Liturgy*; and although it is not perfect (and of course people are great at letting you know what they perceive its faults to be), it does appear to have enabled the church to leave behind much of the divisiveness symbolized by whether a church was a "blue book church" or a "black book church," and to move forward together, united, into the future.

Devotion: The Relationship between Public and Private Worship

We were determined to produce a book which would have equal capacity to enrich private as well as corporate devotion.

There is always an underlying philosophy which influences the creation of a prayer book. This is often sub-conscious, not least in terms of the relationship between public and private prayer.

The question of how a prayer book is seen is also focussed by the development of new ways of presenting liturgy. The question is asked, and certainly was asked in the Irish context, about how much longer we would be using worship books as such. It is clearly possible to make liturgies available by electronic means (and the Irish edition of *Visual Liturgy* does this very effectively, even asking corrective questions of a worship leader such as "Are you sure you want to use the *Gloria* during Lent?"). For many churches the worship sheet or bulletin is the order of the day each Sunday, and it is possible to print out the whole liturgy with variable elements such as hymns, songs, readings, and propers, in course. For other churches, including some in my own diocese, Powerpoint ™ has made it possible to more or less dispense with paper altogether, and to put everything on a big screen, or even thin plasma monitors carefully placed around the church.

So why do we still need books?

The question is answered in a variety of ways. For some, the raison d'etre for the book itself has changed. This is true of the Church of England's *Common Worship. Common Worship*, it is claimed, is not a book, but a series of books. The basic book is one that contains liturgical material for Sundays, principal feasts, and holy days, but there is also a *Pastoral Services* book, a *Daily Office* book, and a *Times and Seasons* book. Alongside these are many materials for Services of the Word in *New Patterns for Worship*. The situation can sometimes be like the old pre-reformation "Pie" with its many directions for worship — taking longer to find the right materials for the services than actually to conduct them!

In this model of liturgy, of course, the books do not necessarily need to be owned by the ordinary worshipper — they may well be too complex and expensive for that. Instead, nowadays, as I have mentioned and we have experienced, the Sunday worshipper will often have a sheet, or a booklet, or the liturgy compiled from resources available electronically. This model allows for a richness of liturgical material and options to be available, but distances accessibility to much of the material from the ordinary worshipper, and may well, over a period of time, have an effect on how much memorable material is stored in worshippers' minds.

Others may answer the question "Why do we still need books?" by declaring that the whole idea of having or even owning a prayer book is part of the genius of Anglicanism — at least since printing became relatively inexpensive. It has often been declared that the *Book of Common Prayer* held the Anglican Communion together over many centuries, usually without the realization that there has never solely been one *Book of Common Prayer*. This can be illustrated simply by asking how many of you here in the United States know instinctively the 1662 *Book of Common Prayer*, which of course provides the roots of the traditional services used in Ireland? The answer is probably very few indeed, because your roots are in the 1637 *Book of Common Prayer*, and your traditional liturgies have developed from there. We will come back to this in a later section of the lecture.

It is, however, undoubtedly true that the whole idea of a prayer book has been central in Anglican thinking. I remember very powerfully a visit from Robert Runcie, Archbishop of Canterbury at the time, to the International Anglican Youth Congress held in Belfast in 1988. There he shared the view that instead of exporting the idea of liturgical worship to Africa, the Church of England had managed to export the precise book itself, with all the English accoutrements of hymnody, vesture, etc., duly attached. What perhaps needs to be remembered is that the

Reformation took place in England just at the point when printing was taking off, so the association between the dissemination of Reformed doctrine in liturgy and printing was particularly close. Perhaps today's Cranmer would be more inclined to use electronic dissemination of material!

However, there is another view, which lies at the heart of the decision of the Church of Ireland to produce a new prayer book on what is essentially the old model—that is, that all the material for the chief acts of worship, Office, Eucharist, initiation, pastoral services, ordination, etc., would be available in one volume for the whole people of God. It is summed up in these points:

• With all the new forms of publishing, people still like to have a book. In fact sales of books are higher than ever, and this has proved to be the case with the new Book of Common Prayer.

• People also like to have a book that looks and "feels" like a book of personal devotion. So, in our Irish revision we have paid attention to layout, to a classical print style, to red rubrics, to size, weight, markers, and paper. As one reviewer said: "It feels like a book of devotion."

• It is important, if a Book of Common Prayer is to bring about commonality, that everyone should have easy access to it. Of course this was not possible in Cranmer's day when books were large and printing costly, but it became the norm in the Church of Ireland that every person, or at least family, should have their own prayer book. The Book of Common Prayer must be seen as one of those books you have to own, to be presented in attractive ways for gifts, etc.

• It must be useable for daily prayers (and you will notice that the book begins with a structure for simple daily prayer in the inside cover, and structured daily intercessions), with actual memorable prayers in it, with an easily usable Psalter and Canticles, and with the lectionary laid out in such a way that people can prepare for Sunday worship. It must also be possible for those who come to baptism, confirmation, marriage, and funerals to know that they can go to the book and prepare by knowing and understanding the liturgy, and for those who are sick to find spiritual comfort in it.

All of this is brought home to a pastor most powerfully when visiting someone who is ill at home or in hospital, and finding beside the bed a Bible and Prayer Book. This brings the realization that, for many, these have been the books which have structured and sustained their walk with God, and we have the duty and privilege of enabling that to continue. The creative juices of liturgists, with their endless pursuit of new liturgies—many of which only they themselves are seeking—need to be restrained when developing what is the common private and public prayer of the people of God.

Faith: Lex orandi, lex credendi

We desired that this book, like previous editions of it, should properly articulate and embody the Church's faith.

Geoffrey Wainwright, in his magisterial book *Doxology*, rightly notes that the Latin tag *Lex orandi, lex credendi* may be construed in two ways. He says: "The more usual way makes the rule of prayer a norm for belief; what is prayed indicates what may and must be believed. But from the grammatical point of view it is equally possible to reverse subject and predicate and so take the tag as meaning that the rule of faith is the norm for prayer: what must be believed governs what may and should be prayed."

The 2004 *Book of Common Prayer* acts as though the tag really does work both ways. There has been a carefulness about the wording of worship because of the fact that it is a vehicle for the expression and teaching of doctrine, and the teaching of pure doctrine is important. This has always been the case. So, when the revision of the *Book of Common Prayer* was taking place in the 1870s after the disestablishment of the Church of Ireland, there were many contentious arguments about doctrinal issues such as prayers for the departed, baptismal regeneration, the nature of Christ's presence in the Eucharist, and the priest's "Ego te absolvo" in the ministry to the sick. When the Church of Ireland argues about doctrine, it often argues from the Prayer Book first and from the scriptures second! This in itself is a recognition of the vital importance of the words that are used in worship.

What we have to realize, of course, is that on this front many of the contemporary liturgies of the 2004 *Book of Common Prayer* are categorically different to the traditional liturgies, and, although they are not intended to reject any former doctrine or indeed teach new doctrine, they approach the matter from a different angle. In general, the implicit agreement that the Liturgical Advisory Committee made with the General Synod was that the traditional "thee-form" liturgies from the 1926 *Book of Common Prayer* would remain the same as they had always been. Congregations should notice no difference. This was both because of the desire on the part of some to worship in the well-worn, familiar ways, and also because of the realization that the Prayer Book embodies our theology. The only changes were intended to be small verbal ones, such as "Ghost" being changed to "Spirit," and a clearer and more easily followed layout. In terms of the latter, it soon became clear to the Liturgical Advisory Committee that even the most minor rubrical changes can imply a change in doctrine and open up a can of worms. Let me offer two examples:

• In Morning and Evening Prayer, the rubric before the absolution in 1926 said: *The Absolution or Remission of sins, to be pronounced by the Priest alone, standing; the people still kneeling.* This has been simplified in 2004 to say: *The Absolution or Remission of sins is pronounced by the priest alone.* The question is, does the change imply that only the priest can say it (whereas it could be argued that Cranmer used priest and minister interchangeably), rather than that the priest alone is standing?

• In Holy Communion, the rubric before the first Lord's Prayer in 1926 was simply, *The minister shall say the service following in a distinct and audible voice.* A rubric was suggested stating that the priest alone say the first Lord's Prayer, following on from a romantic Victorian custom that this was the last part of the priest's private devotion. That rubric might have been true to custom in most places, but would have been a particular interpretation of the doctrine of the Prayer Book.

I am aware that those examples are a bit like the Pharisees straining at gnats, but they do nevertheless provide examples of how even apparently harmless rubrical changes in a very carefully considered and dense text can provide the basis for a change in teaching and understanding. It is also important to note that some services have been included in the new prayer book which will rarely, and in some cases possibly never, be used (e.g., the traditional forms of baptism, confirmation, and ordination). They are present, as much as anything, because they have a role in establishing foundational doctrine.

With the more contemporary liturgies almost the opposite is the case. These liturgies have carefully been "opened up" to allow for a much wider flexibility. In *Holy Communion Two* (*One* is used for traditional liturgies, *Two* for contemporary), the opening prayer is "up for grabs," penitence can be conducted in different ways, the intercessions can be the creation of the person praying, and many parts of the service can be omitted on various occasions. In *A Late Evening Office* there is provision for open prayer, where it is in reality impossible to control the orthodoxy or heterodoxy of the prayers.

A Service of the Word is basically a structure in which nearly anything can happen. While it is true to say that at least no heresy which may be uttered is in print, we do need to be aware that people's doctrine can and will be formed by what they hear in public worship, for the better or for the worse.

The 2004 *Book of Common Prayer* also

provides doctrinal statements that are controls on teaching in the church. It is important at this point to note that the Thirty-nine Articles are not included in the new prayer book simply as an historic document. In fact such a heading was rejected by the Liturgical Advisory Committee. They are included within the context of the Preamble and Declaration adopted by the General Convention of the Church of Ireland at disestablishment in 1870 which states: "The Church of Ireland doth receive and approve the Book of the Articles of Religion, commonly called the Thirty-nine articles." All clergypersons are required, at key points in their ministry, to make the Declarations that state: "I assent to the Thirty-nine Articles of Religion, and to the Book of Common Prayer and of the Ordering of Bishops, Priests and Deacons. I believe the doctrine of the Church of Ireland, as therein set forth …"

Having said that, the Church of Ireland, in General Synod, did make a statement about the kind of language used in some of the Articles in relation to other Christian churches, while discussing the issues of sectarianism in our society. While affirming the Articles, it was stated: "Negative statements towards other Christians should not be seen as representing the spirit of this church today," and it continues: "The Church of Ireland regrets that words written in another age and in a different context, should be used in a manner hurtful to or antagonistic towards, other Christians."

The other doctrinal statements of the 2004 *Book of Common Prayer* are the Athanasian Creed (which has not been required in public worship since 1878, but is still accepted as one of the three historic creeds), and the 1878 Catechism.

You have asked me to lecture today specifically on the Church of Ireland's 2004 *Book of Common Prayer*, and it may be useful, under this doctrinal section, to return to some of the issues that have traditionally been contentious in what was historically a very "protestant" church. You will find in this prayer book, for example,

a restraint in terms of prayers for the departed, which are limited mostly to remembrance and thanksgiving; you will find a carefulness about explicating doctrine with regard to the presence of Christ in the Eucharist. For example, the Church of England prayer: "Almighty God, we thank you for feeding us with the body and blood of your Son Jesus Christ …" is amended to read: "the spiritual food of the body and blood …" You will also discover a reticence about sacrificial language in the Eucharist other than the one sacrifice of Christ once and for all, as distinguished from the sacrifice of praise and thanksgiving and our responsive sacrifice of "ourselves, our souls and bodies." And you will find a care taken about how the epiclesis is expressed in the eucharistic prayers. It is not seen as an epiclesis on the bread and wine but rather as being on the whole event and body of worshippers.

The use of language of regeneration in baptism has been slightly mellowed, allowing in one of the services for the omission of a prayer after baptism claiming regeneration. You will find also no reference to August 15; and this prayer book contains perhaps the only modern Ash Wednesday Service in Anglicanism with no ashes! Reference to such a custom might divide.

All of this will give you some insight into the Church of Ireland, its context, its background, and the way it will seek to stay united across theological differences generally by finding a restrained way forward, and the continuing important use of the prayer book in passing on the teaching of the church to future generations, and in protecting against wrong teaching.

Communion: Worldwide Catholicity

We hoped that the book would strengthen the bonds of unity with sister churches who share our approach to common prayer, and we were therefore fully attentive to the reports of the successive meetings of the International Anglican Liturgical Consultation.

The Preface to the 2004 Church of Ireland *Book of Common Prayer* is probably the first in the Anglican Communion to mention the International Anglican Liturgical Consultations. I probably do not need to go into the history of these consultations because Bryan Spinks has been very involved over the years, and will no doubt have kept you up-to-date. At this point I will simply say that they began in 1987 when a group of Anglicans who were members of *Societas Liturgica* met to discuss the issue of children and communion, and issued the Boston Statement. The Church of Ireland discussed the issue and did not go down the line of the Boston Statement. In fact, the only change on this front liturgically was the agreement of General Synod to open up slightly the possibility of children receiving communion by changing the confirmation rubric from: "Every person ought to present himself for Confirmation (unless prevented by some urgent reason) before he partakes of the Lord's Supper" to what was in fact the older English wording of 1662: "And there shall none be admitted to the Holy Communion, until such time as *he* be confirmed, or be ready and desirous to be confirmed." The reason for this change was to open the door slightly by using traditional wording and without dividing the synod, which was a real possibility on this issue.

Having said that, the Church of Ireland has, however, been profoundly influenced by IALCs since then, at most of which I have had the privilege of being present. The major work of the IALCs in the nineties and early part of this decade has been to respond to the three key areas of the Lima Statement: baptism, Eucharist and ministry. This led to a statement on baptism (Toronto, 1991), on the Eucharist (Dublin, 1995), and on ordination (Berkeley, 2001). Each of these statements developed an understanding of the liturgies concerned, and also a suggested structure for those services; these are generally adopted as the starting-points for the revision of the Church of Ireland in each of these three areas. The contemporary services in the 2004

Book of Common Prayer which relate to these areas are, therefore, the places of most change and creativity. In using the suggested structure of the IALC it is hoped that we will have liturgies that are essentially in line with other revised liturgies in the communion, at least in terms of shape and ethos. Whether, of course, shape and ethos will prove to be enough to hold us together liturgically in communion at times of stormy waters remains to be seen.

To take these three key areas one by one, and make some brief comments:

Baptism. One of the key themes of the statement on initiation is quite simply that baptism is baptism is baptism. The one liturgy, therefore, should cover baptism, whether it is for infants, children, or adults. Yet another emphasis is that there should be a baptismal quality about the whole service. Another is that additional symbolic actions associated with baptism (in Ireland, the signing with the cross and the giving of a candle) should not be placed in such a way, or given such a weight, as to detract from the water of baptism, which should be administered in quantities large enough to have an impact, with a preference for submersion.

Eucharist. The key structure for the Eucharist was seen as being a fivefold structure with specific headings given. These are: The Gathering of God's People; Proclaiming and Receiving the Word; The Prayers of the People; Celebrating at the Lord's Table; Going out as God's People.

The Word and Table were to be given the major weight, but the priestly ministry of the people of God in prayer was to be seen as of greater importance than hitherto. It might be noticed also that the Church of Ireland's rite two allows for three eucharistic prayers, widening the variety with a new responsive prayer, developed on a Trinitarian model from the English *Common Worship* Prayer H. It needs to be remembered that the Church of Ireland norm is still weekly communion early Sunday morning, communion once a month at the main morning service, and once a month at the main evening service, so a wider variety of eucharistic prayers, as commonly available in other parts of the communion, is not felt necessary at the moment.

Ministry. In the early stages of revision, when the Ordinal was being revised to be placed in *Alternative Occasional Services* (a volume of occasional services in the *Alternative Prayer Book* mode published in 1993), the House of Bishops of the Church of Ireland kept holding up the development of the Ordinal. They seemed to fear the omission of the imperative formula in ordination ("Receive the Holy Ghost …"; "Take thou authority …"). So, the Church of Ireland, which had become the first church in the British Isles to ordain women to the priesthood in the early 1990s, was in fact ordaining them according to what was essentially Cranmer's ordinal (to which inclusive language had to be added!). We were the last of the Anglican churches in the British Isles to have a new ordinal.

I am glad to say that the reverse happened ten years later. Simply because of the timing of the IALC statement we became the first part of the communion to revise our ordinal in the light of Berkeley 2001, perhaps for the first time without looking over our shoulder at the Church of England! You can see the results in the prayer book, and I hope you will be pleased by them.

At this point, it is also worth noting other key factors that tie the 2004 *Book of Common Prayer* into the wider communion and worldwide church, and in which we have greatly benefited from work done here in the United States:

• First is the work of ELLC (The English Language Liturgical Consultation). Sadly, the Roman Catholic Church has been disentangling itself from this consultation, and looks as though it will be doing its own thing in the English translation of the Mass. At an early stage the Liturgical Advisory Committee decided that it would present to the General Synod the ELLC texts, even if we did not altogether like them, for the sake of commonality throughout the world. The 2004 *Book of Common Prayer* has therefore adopted those texts, with variations in only two (these came as amendments from the floor of General Synod). They are the Nicene Creed (in the line: "Was incarnate by the Holy Spirit of the Virgin Mary and was made man") and the Lord's Prayer ("Lead us not into temptation"). The Church of Ireland texts are, therefore, closer to ELLC than those of the Church of England, especially in relation to inclusive language.

• Second, the *Revised Common Lectionary.* As you will probably be aware, the RCL is essentially the work of the Consultation on Common Texts, which originated in the 1960s as a forum for consultation on the renewal of worship among many Christian churches in North America. The roots of this lectionary, are, of course the Roman *Lectionary for Mass* of 1969. It has, however, developed through several stages, all since your last Prayer Book in ECUSA, which of course has the same roots. The main developments were published as the *Common Lectionary* of 1983, and then further as the *Revised Common Lectionary* of 1992. Its main new contribution is to provide an alternative series of semicontinuous readings for Sundays in ordinary time, so that the Old Testament is not read simply as a type of the Gospel. The RCL has been receiving pretty universal support in the English-speaking world. However, sadly, it has not been adopted by Rome. It might also be worth noting that the 2004 *Book of Common Prayer* does not contain a weekday lectionary. The reason is simple: there are a variety of models around, including the new RCL Weekday Lectionary, which is a Thursday to Wednesday lectionary, preparing for and developing from each Sunday's readings. These are too much "up in the air" at the moment, and are produced separately for each year.

• Third, the Psalter. You will notice, if you look carefully at the 2004 Church of Ireland Prayer Book, that there is only one Psalter. At first that may not seem unusual. Your Prayer Book is the same. But when the plans were drawn up for the 2004 BCP, the General Synod was promised two Psalters, one the Coverdale Psalter adapted as in the 1926 book, and the other a contemporary Psalter. The way that plan changed is a reminder of the very ordinary factors that can influence liturgical revision. In the year 2000 the fifth edition of the *Church Hymnal* was produced by Oxford University Press. It is an excellent compilation of hymns, even if I say it myself as someone who was involved in its production. When it was produced the paper weight was much thicker and heavier than anyone had expected, and the church press was full of complaints about "the weight of the new hymnbook" — so much so that no one seemed to notice the contents! In the light of this controversy the Liturgical Advisory Committee thought it wise to re-visit the idea of two Psalters, which could have made the Prayer Book quite bulky. The Synod was given the original two-fold option, or the option of an "in-between" Psalter, that is, with a traditional feel but a little more contemporary. They went for the latter, and the Psalter chosen was the Church of England *Common Worship* Psalter. You will recognize much of it because its roots are in your own Psalter in the ECUSA Prayer Book.

I've spoke of the commonality of prayer, of the relationship between public and private worship, of *lex orandi, lex credendi,* of worldwide catholicity, and given you some keys to understanding the 2004 *Book of Common Prayer* of the Church of Ireland. To finish, I will read just one further section from the 2004 Preface:

> We must always remind ourselves that words, however memorable, beautiful or useful, are never to be confused with worship itself. The words set out on these pages are but the beginning of worship. They need to be appropriated with care and devotion by the People of God so that, with the aid of the Holy Spirit, men and women may bring glory to the Father and grow in the knowledge and likeness of Jesus Christ.

When I was a rector of a parish in Cork, we once had a worship sub-committee. It had only one question to ask and answer, and the question was this: "What one thing about worship must we get right?" In other words, what matters most? Is it the preaching, the music, the ritual, the centrality of the Eucharist, inculturation, atmosphere, a sense of the numinous, or what? Well, after three meetings the committee answered in one word: *integrity.* The word was defined like this: The inside and the outside must be the same. How we look should be how we are. The wholeheartedness of our worship should be expressed wholeheartedly; words should have meaning and the meaning should be seen in our lives, so that we are the same people from Monday to Saturday as we are on Sunday. When the words and rituals of our liturgies express and form the worship of our hearts, then we are truly blessed. When the words of a Prayer Book are incarnated in the life of a Christian community, then we are dangerous in a godly way. When the written word draws us to the living Word, and changes our lives, we are on to a winner — because true worship in the scriptures is never just liturgical actions, but the whole of what it means to love God with all our heart and soul and mind and strength, and our neighbors as ourselves.

Harold Miller is Bishop of Down and Dromore in Northern Ireland. He has been involved in liturgy for several decades, being the first member of the Church of Ireland to be involved in the International Anglican Liturgical Consultations. At the moment he chairs the Liturgical Advisory Committee of the Church of Ireland. He has written several books and booklets on liturgical matters, the most recent being The Desire of Our Soul *(Columbia, 2004), and has contributed to the* Oxford Guide to the Book of Common Prayer, *published in 2006. He is married to Liz and has four children.*

Music and Culture

Penderecki at the Beinecke Library

The Tangeman Lecture delivered as a preconcert interview
before a performance of the composer's Credo, *April 22, 2005*

Good evening. I'm Greg Dubinsky, lecturer in history at the Yale School of Music. Maestro Penderecki, could you tell us something about the genesis of the Credo *that you're going to perform this evening.*

Yes. It's a pretty long story. Almost twenty-five years ago Helmuth Rilling, director of the Oregon Bach Festival, asked me to write a new piece, a new sacred work. It took many, many years because I was engaged in other pieces. In my first talk with him I wanted to write a Christmas oratorio, which I gave up after a couple of months. Then a *Stabat Mater*—I had written a *Stabat Mater* a capella earlier, but this time it was supposed to be a piece with soloists and choir and orchestra. Then we landed on the idea that I would write a Mass. In my long list of sacred works I never wrote a Mass, really. So I agreed, and after another very large-scale piece, *Seven Days of Jerusalem,* which I finished in 1996, I decided I would now start the Mass, and maybe it would be my last sacred work.

So I started the Mass. I started it with the Sanctus and with the Kyrie, the Agnus Dei; I was afraid to start the Credo, because the Credo is not a text that can immediately inspire a composer. I remember that this was in February, and the first performance was to be in August, in Oregon. In February I started the Credo because I thought that if I did not write it now there would be a Mass without a Credo. There are some Masses like that. I started, and the Credo grew and grew. I forgot about the other movements. After the Credo was an hour long I decided that I was not going to continue with the other movements. Maybe my *Credo* is the longest Credo ever written.

How did you approach the Credo text? I noticed

you've added some texts to the traditional words.

Yes. The text is a rather dry text. I was looking for some literature, of course sacred literature. I took other texts like the *Commentary to the Credo*, especially from the Holy Week liturgy, and also others like apocalypses. There are many short but important texts that made this form possible

Did they start to amplify or describe?

Yes, to sometimes edit a text that is dry with some other poetic text.

When I was listening to this work I noticed that you also repeat texts at various points. This is a work of very symphonic dimensions.

Yes, of course, but this is something that all composers do. There are some pieces like the Bach *Amen* that take maybe five minutes—and it's only "Amen." So of course I do repeat. Yes, this piece has a symphonic form. The end of the piece is like a romantic idea, to bring all the subjects together in a finale, to finish.

The end of this Credo *I find quite striking. I find your approach to this Credo text overall, in terms of the dramaturgy of the Credo, much different from Credos we might know.*

Yes, at that time I was very late. I am a composer who delivers a piece sometimes a couple of days before the performance. This time it was the same. A week before the first performance, actually it was in July, not in August, a week before the performance I finished the last page. In Oregon, I was writing. And I knew, of course, that it's only the Credo, so it has to have a grand finale. And it does. Of course, this is a different kind of Credo from what other composers did, which is only one movement. Here it is the entire piece, with a closed form.

I find the tenor—the tone of this music—for the last half of this Credo *rather surprising in some respects, and much different from previous settings. The* Resurrexit, *which you set, and the* Et vitam venturi saeculi, *texts that have been set by composers in a very joyful manor, with bright major fugues, have a much different flavor under your pen. Would you care to …*

Ah, yes. Of course, the *Resurrexit.* There are two movements that are almost similar, by all the composers. These are the *Crucifixus,* of course, which is the central movement in this piece. It has been greatly influenced by Bach, by the *B Minor Mass.* That was maybe my real inspiration. The *Resurrexit,* that's the only fragment that allows the movement to ride to allegro or presto. In such a long piece, which is an hour long, I made use of this text, adding, of course, some things, especially from apocalypses …

I find this apocalyptic tone to be very, very striking, and very, very impressive. It has some unusual sounds in it, as well. Is there anything…

You mean the instruments? I'm always looking for new instruments. For one hundred years we have not had really new instruments; we have to use the same—almost the same—instruments as composers one hundred years ago did. Maybe the newest instrument we use is the saxophone, which is over a hundred years old. So in each piece I try to introduce a new instrument. In this case the percussion instrument I used is the boobam [an idiophone composed of bamboo tubes]. The boobam is the percussion instrument closest to the marimba, but more striking. I think it's a fantastic instrument, and the player, he is excellent.

Where did you find this boobam?

I have a very good friend who is the producer of percussion instruments. Sometimes I visit him and he shows me some instruments.

Have you used some of his other instruments before, or is this the first time?

In *The Seven Days of Jerusalem* I used tuba-phones, [which are] also percussion instruments. They are new instruments, never used before. Long tubes. They allowed me to go very low, to A-flat sub-contra [two octaves below bass clef staff]; no other instrument can really use this range.

That's remarkable. It [the boobam] makes an appearance again near the end of the Credo; *when talking about sins and so forth this material returns. As I was listening what particularly struck me about your* Credo *is the very opening of this piece. When the text talks about* Dominum Jesum Christum *and* Filium Dei *you have almost ecstatic music, bright triumphs, soaring very, very high. Perhaps it is promising an ending for this composition that will be equally bright and affirmative. And what strikes me about the last third or so of this piece is the degree to which the tone stays stoic; there is a lot of lamenting and anguish, and that tone remains present except at the very end when you have the extraordinary effect of the chorus. They have been singing in minor chords and with open fifths, but they disappear, and then as if from a distance a major triad suddenly appears, bringing just a little ray of hope to what had been a fairly anguished* Credo. *I wonder if you can say something about this.*

I don't know, because I am always writing a piece as a whole. I'm not a composer who sees the piano and plays some chords. The concept is, from the beginning, thinking of the whole piece. And of course I have high points connected with the text, but sometimes not, sometimes connected with the music, which is even more important, I think. I am sometimes only using the text while writing my music. The music goes and the text follows. This many composers did, I think, before me; it's nothing new. But this is maybe the only way to overwhelm the large form.

Czesław Miłosz, the Polish poet, has said that he felt that one of the almost defining characteristics of Polish poetry, especially after the Second World War, and of Polish literature, is what he sometimes terms catastrophism — in other words, an awareness of either impending doom, or of the precariousness of everyday life. He said that one of the great contributions that Polish art has made since the Second World War is that because Poland has been through so much history its art serves as a great witness to that. Do you feel that at all?

Yes, of course. It happens that I lived through the War, and then the long, long, dark Russian occupation. There was not much space for light and hope sometimes, only despair. So it's not only Polish literature, Russian is the same, and Czech, and all of the Eastern European literatures, behind the Iron Curtain. And the music. And of course Slavic music is more dramatic and personal when compared to Western music. Very romantic. I was very much aware of where I was living. I wrote some pieces that are very much connected to that history that I witnessed. In 1959 I wrote *Threnody for the Victims of Hiroshima*, and then the *Auschwitz Oratorio* in 1967. *The Passion according to St. Luke* is not only the passion of Christ, it is a very dramatic work. And other pieces, of course, because of the place. If I lived in New Zealand, maybe my music would be completely different.

I'm sorry for my voice, because I caught a cold, and I am happy that I am conducting and not singing tonight.

Speaking of conducting, you do conduct a great deal. Is that important for you as a composer?

Yes. I learn a lot, much more than you learn in a school, conducting. Because I deal with live musicians, not with a computer, fortunately. And they give me…always, it is a source of inspiration for me, working with an orchestra. And of course there is something that I will always say, that the composition is much richer and bigger in the imagination than the composer is able to really write. This happens in each piece I am writing: I think I could have written it much better than I did, but there is no way…and something is lost during working. But conducting, especially if there is a good acoustic, a good

orchestra and choir and soloists, then I can bring it back, something that has been lost. Some atmosphere, some color of the orchestra. So there is always excitement in recreating the piece once more, and again and again. This is important for the composer. In the past almost all the composers we know were also conducting, with few exceptions.

As a performer as well as a composer you occupy yourself a great deal with the music of the past, and it keeps percolating up through your music. I've noticed in different interviews that you've given over the years that the composers who are very important to you change with the times. Bach, and then Ockeghem…

Bach is staying always. I change other composers, but never Bach.

So who are you taking a fresh look at nowadays, composers that you've maybe enjoyed in the past but who all of a sudden seem much more…

Sorry to say, but I prefer always the past, and the distant past sometimes to the contemporary. Of course some composers of the twentieth century have been very influential in my music. Certainly Stravinsky, Bartok, Olivier Messiaen. Not so many, actually. But always I find inspiration in Beethoven's music, and of course Bach, Monteverdi, sixteenth-century polyphony. I think this is the most important for me, the inspiration. I'm forgetting — of course there was a period, maybe a short one, when I was very much inspired by, for example, Bruckner, Mahler, but maybe more Bruckner. In that time I wrote my *Christmas Symphony Number 2.*

You've been composing many, many symphonies, especially in the 1990s. I think you're completing symphony number eight now.

I'm here, in New Haven.

I'm noticing certain sorts of parallels in your thought. Many of your works deal with giant cosmological themes: apocalypse, redemption. You're very interested in large symphonic forms — large works that sort of have a beginning, a genesis, and movement through to an end, that are sort of a world unto themselves. I also realize you've created a personal world all for yourself at your home...

Yes, every five or seven years I take a sabbatical, and write music that I really like, which is chamber music. This is a fantastic time for me. In 1999 and 2000 I wrote two large chamber works—this is always very personal music. It's my *musica domestica*. And they were written in my country house, quiet, in my park. I don't know if you know this—I'm very much interested, and I started an arboretum at my country house. It's a big park, over six hectares, fifteen hundred species of trees. This is my passion after music. Sometimes in the spring I plant the trees maybe even more than music. In my asylum there I am writing chamber music. This is the place where I feel in the mood to write very personal music.

We have just a little time left. If I might ask you one final question. In the 1970s you taught here at Yale at the School of Music. Do you have any recollection, fond recollections, of your time in New Haven, or any remarks about that?

Yes, I was writing here very important pieces, like the *First Violin Concerto* for Isaac Stern. I wrote here *Paradise Lost*. Many, many pieces. I must say that now after working with the orchestra and choir and soloists here I think that almost thirty years later there has been enormous progress in the level of the young musicians. Working with them is really a pleasure, no problem at all. They're very open, technically fantastic. I don't think I could have done thirty years ago such a concert as I hope will be tonight.

We're all in great anticipation of this concert tonight. Thank you very much.

his compositional style has reflected the evolution of new music from the avant-garde of the 1960s up to the present day, through which time he has preserved his own distinctive voice. He is the recipient of numerous awards, prizes, and honorary degrees, and is an honorary member of the Royal Academy of Music in London, the Royal Academy of Music in Dublin, the Accademia di Santa Cecilia in Rome, the Royal Academy of Music in Stockholm, and the Adademie der Künste in Berlin, and bears the Order of Merit of the Federal Republic of Germany and the designation Freeman of the City of Strasbourg.

Born in Debica, Poland, in 1933, Krzysztof Penderecki is one of the most esteemed and widely discussed composers of our time. The development of

Messiaen, Saint Francis, and the Birds of Faith

CHARLES H. J. PELTZ

*I have been asked to deliver a confession of my
faith, that is, to talk about what I believe, what
I love, what I hope for. What do I believe? That
doesn't take long to say and in it everything is said
at once: I believe in God. And because I believe
in God I believe likewise in the Holy Trinity and
[especially] the Holy Spirit.*[1]

I have read that quotation many times and I am
still astounded. I am astounded by the strength
in its delivery and the personal submission in its
substance. Olivier Messiaen offered it in 1971 to
assembled dignitaries upon receipt of the Praemium Erasmianum, an honor acknowledging his
status as an artist. Like the irresistible utterances
of truth by Daniel to the Babylonians, Paul to
the Corinthians, and Christ to the Pharisees, the
words were out of fashion for both the moment
and the era. As with his biblical predecessors, the
career risks were high for a musician of his stat-
ure to openly proclaim God. His age was not one
of sorting through conflicting passions about
God's truth. Rather it was a century of hoping
that God would evaporate through disinterest,
wherein musicians spent great energy denying
the Gott of "Götterfunken."

    A composer of some of the twentieth cen-
tury's most important works, Messiaen was both
a giant of music and a devout Christian Catholic
apologist. His was a highly original voice marked
by an extraordinary use of time and its active
offspring, rhythm, and a use of color more vivid
than one could have imagined even with his
French birthright of iridescent sound. Moreover,
Messiaen synthesized rhetorics from the most
basic found in nature to the most advanced
created by humans, a synthesis so potent and
perfect that it makes the resultant new language
awesomely clear in its ability to communicate
the essence of life.

    Messiaen communicated religious ideas

through this new musical language, and so his
work is best seen as an expression of evangelism.
One of Messiaen's evangelical inspirations was
Saint Francis of Assisi, whose life inspired the
opera that bears the saint's name. By examining each man and his work in light of the other
we can illumine that which "touches all things
without ceasing to touch God."[2]

    Born in 1908 in Avignon, Olivier Messi-
aen was the child of two highly literary parents:
his father, Pierre, was a scholar and teacher
whose work included extensive translations of
Shakespeare; his mother, Cecile Sauvage, was
a noted poet. By age eight he had memorized
great chunks of Shakespeare and Tennyson,
whose work he described in adulthood as "su-
perfairytales."[3] Self-taught at the piano, he was
compelled by his insatiable musical curiosity to
beg for scores of Gluck, Wagner, and Mozart as
Christmas gifts, and at age nine he composed
his first work, *Le Dame de Shallot*. By age eleven
he was attending the Paris Conservatory, where
for the next eleven years he studied the whole
of music from an array of notable teachers,
including Dupré and Dukas.[4] Although the Prix
de Rome eluded him, he received virtually all
of the Conservatory's honors. In 1930 he left the
Conservatory, and one year later accepted the
post of organist at La Trinité in Paris, a position
he would hold for more than sixty years.

    In 1941, after being captured and impris-
oned by the Nazis, he wrote in a Silesian stalag
his first great work, *Quartet for the End of Time*,
depicting the apocalypse from the book of
Revelation. Performed in the prison camp for an
audience of five thousand enthralled prison-
ers, this work for clarinet, violin, cello, and
piano was a groundbreaking work, a dramatic
synthesis of Messiaen's religiously inspired ideas
and musical language.[5] After his release from the
prison camp in 1942, he returned to Paris and

an appointment to the Paris Conservatory. His well known students included Boulez, Xenakis, and Stockhausen. The intensity of these musical rebels contrasted greatly with the serenity of Père Messiaen.

Messiaen's musical life unfolded over the next fifty years through compositions for chorus, orchestra (including the sprawling musical landscape *Turangulila–Symphony*), wind and brass ensemble, and organ. All these works culminated in the opera *Saint Francis* (1975–1983), a work of Wagnerian proportions based upon central moments in the life of the Umbrian saint. Messiaen's compositional style evolved over those fifty years, but changed direction very little. As he said about music over the ages, "The music of our time is quite a natural continuation of the music of the past; doubtless there are changes, but no rupture."[6] His musical path was similar: he adopted various techniques, including aleatory and serialism, but remained faithful to his unique synthesis of languages.

Imagine being a child whose mother writes this as she carries you in her womb: "I carry within me the love of mysterious and marvelous things."[7] It is what Cecile wrote in a volume of poems to her unborn son titled *L'âme en Bourgeon*. It seems inevitable that the son of such literary parents would in some "mysterious and marvelous" way find language the fuel for his creative engine.[8] Messiaen created his own fuel, his own language, by interweaving musical language with the languages of many living beings.

Birdsong

Oiseaux exotiques, the *Exotic Birds*, was composed in 1956. That same year, coincidentally, the English edition of Messiaen's book *Technique de mon langage musical* was published. Written in 1944, this handbook explains the sources and thoughts behind the musical phenomena he created, and it is an invaluable aid in understanding them. He makes clear that this is not a book on how to compose, but rather a guide to the "rhythmic,

melodic and harmonic" views of his music.[9] In addition to this trinity of musical elements, he describes his use of Hindu and Greek rhythms and of birdsongs, influences that figure prominently in *Oiseaux*.

Birds were the world's first musicians, or so goes the cliché. In chapter 9 of *Technique*, Messiaen quoted Dukas: "Listen to the birds! They are great masters." It is to these first musicians that Messiaen turned reflexively for both spiritual inspiration and direct musical material. He collected bird song, as Bartok and Grainger collected folk songs, with an obsession for accuracy. His passion was to notate the primary source, and thereby insure fidelity to that source when recreated by humans. Unlike the nightingale and cuckoo of Beethoven's *Pastoral Symphony*, idealized birds à la Watteau, he collected real birds from around the world and unleashed them, à la Hitchcock, in the concert hall: *Musique vérité*.

Now arises one of those heat-creating and light-discouraging arguments that divert the best discourse. Did Messiaen really transcribe birdsong with complete accuracy? Would a cardinal rush inquisitively (or passionately?) to the room of a clarinetist practicing Messiaen? (Quite an image: the two of them—beak to bell—in doomed unrequitedness.) Some assert they can prove (by scientific/acoustical comparisons) that Messiaen was uncannily accurate in the process of transcribing; others think that he fell markedly away from fidelity. Messiaen himself addressed this debate. He said, "I'd like to talk about the musical forms in which I use birdsongs. There are two different forms, one deceitful and one truthful. The deceitful one employs the birdcalls as raw material after the manner of composers of electronic music, who use birdsongs as a source which they constantly electronically alter."[10]

Matthew Gurewitsch offers a brilliant insight into the near impossibility of a wholly "truthful" collection and notation:

> Birds do not sing the way people write music, and transcribing them was like

concocting algebra to reproduce calligraphy: it took creativity of no small order. Birdsong moves faster than human fingers; the first thing to go when an instrumentalist mimics a bird is tempo. Also, Western melodies are strung together from notes, well-defined pitches neatly arrayed on scales. Birds sing microtones. Their staccato "notes" are more like jagged shards than human musicians' points and beads of sound. The timbres and attacks are often energetic to the point of harshness, yet to our ears in the wild they may sound ineffably sweet. For the piano and for instruments of the orchestra Messiaen invented ways of clustering and combining notes to produce, often with uncanny verisimilitude, an impression of the real thing. Call it trompe l'oreille.[11]

The argument about Messiaen's fidelity to nature is an unhelpful and distracting exercise. Gurewitsch articulates the view that complete fidelity to nature is often impossible. Messiaen says that when complete fidelity is possible he is "truthful"; when it is not, he uses the birdsong as primary raw material to be crafted into "trompe l'oreille."

Messiaen realized that sometimes a single instrumental voice could not represent the complex timbres in a bird call. In a 1968 panel discussion he said: "Then comes a further difficulty: the reproduction of timbres. These tone colors are so extraordinary that no musical instrument can reproduce them. One needs combinations of instruments and still more combinations or complexes of pitches."[12] He is not despairing here, nor overwhelmed by the limitations of instruments. Instead he is compelled by the timbral problem to find sonic solutions ranging from the truthfully real to the deceptively surreal. Take for example the piano solo from another piano and orchestral work, *Reveil des oiseaux* (1953). Here the bird song is confined to the treble register, nearer

that of a real birdsong, a reasonably "truthful" choice. On the other hand, a piano excerpt from *Oiseaux* shows Messiaen's use of the bass clef of the piano, a register impossible among birds in nature. Why this surreal extension of range? The answers are manifold, but two may suffice. One answer comes from the composer as artist: an expanded tessitura broadens the musical palette immensely, and that breadth once established can be referred to repeatedly. Another answer comes from the composer as evangelist: a surreal range is possible in a divinely and miraculously recreated nature. Messiaen suspends natural law in order to create a musical version of divine creation, a deeper version God might wish us to hear.

Oiseaux suspends another natural law: these fifty-odd birds, from around the world, would never in nature be found together in one place. They are brought together here by a great human re-creator, their supernatural migration making a more perfect community. Here is a magnificent Christian concept: whether it is the Pentecostal speaking in a multitude of foreign tongues (Acts 2:4) or the uniting of nations as recorded in Matthew 25:32, an invisible Creator brings together all living things in a world perfectly created to inspire declamations of life and joy.

In the twenty-minute *Oiseaux*, Messiaen employs non-birdsong music and from this music creates a world in which his birds exist: his second preface to the piece lists the birds that nest between the double bars of *Oiseaux*. In order to create this aviary he cast the following instruments as birds: solo piano, piccolo, flute, oboe, E-flat clarinet, two B-flat clarinets, bass clarinet, bassoon, two horns, trumpet, glockenspiel, and xylophone. (There are other percussion instruments whose function will be explored later.) He had two reasons for emphasizing winds and excluding strings from this roster. First and most simply, wind instruments create sound as birds do: air activating a vibrating surface. Second—and here Messiaen joins other twentieth-century composers such as Varèse in affirming an unsentimental musical aesthetic—strings have an identity rooted in the sentimental nineteenth century, a romantic and pretty sonic perfume best dissipated by the bracing rush of wind.

Harmony. Messiaen's reference to the need for "complexes of pitches" in addition to "combinations of instruments" opens the door to a discussion of harmony. The melody as sung by any single bird is a horizontal affair. Simultaneous horizontal voices create polyphony, which in turn creates vertical phenomena. Polyphonic phenomena create much of Messiaen's harmony, although vertical harmonies, placed by him independently of counterpoint, are often present. These second harmonies are the branches upon which the birds rest. Messiaen remarked on harmony in the *Technique*: "All these investigations ought not to make us forget the natural harmony: the true, unique, voluptuously pretty by essence, willed by the melody, issued from it, pre-existent in it, having always been enclosed in it, awaiting manifestation."[13] Using this idea Messiaen harmonizes birdsong. He illumines specific birdsongs more than merely accompanies, much like a stage light in which an actor moves. This harmony is "willed" (inspired) "by the melody" (birdsong).

To understand Messiaen's harmony we must look at how he deals with pitch. Messiaen often created "modes of limited transposition"[14] unrelated to the church modes and other scales in common use. The series of half and whole steps in these modes makes up both the melody and harmony when he creates new music. The particular sonority created when certain notes of a mode are stacked on top of one another has multiple implications for Messiaen, of which the first is the unique function of harmony illuminating melodic material, harmony as an essential light and particular color.

An essential point must be made here: Messiaen heard all music in color. "The second

drama [of my life] consists of my telling people that I see colours whenever I hear music, and they see nothing, nothing at all. That's terrible."[15] The modal harmonies are a base color for the music, colors often very specifically described: mode 3 is colored "orange in a halo of milky white, speckled with a little red like an opal"; more prosaically, mode 4 is "dark purple."[16] He changes the base color by "added notes" (his technical term) outside of the mode, often in the order of a sixth, seventh, ninth, and tritone.[17] The addition of these notes results in harmonies that can be narrowly thought of as tone clusters, but, by identifying the essential modal aspects first, we hear these non-mode tones as carefully chosen added tones. There is always a sense that each composite color is a vivid mix, never a sonic "brown" resulting from the indiscriminate piling on of colors/notes.

In *Oiseaux* the modes are used to harmonize many musical moments, especially when the polyphony of birdcalls is less dense. In the first measure we have the call of the mainate hindou in the winds and trumpet. It is a prime example of harmonizing a singular bird call. On the first vertical color in the score we have the pitches C-sharp, D, E-flat, G, A-flat, A. Given in this order we have the interval set 0, 1, 2, 6 (plus added tones of 7 and 8) from mode 4 starting on C-sharp instead of C. If we start with G, A-flat, A, C-sharp, D, E-flat we have 0, 1, 2, 6 (added 7 and 8). This 0, 1, 2, 6 combination will be the basis of much of the vertical material of the piece. In bar two the combination is extended over 2 beats; the added E (9) now is a new color.

This small sample of a harmonic system reveals Messiaen the innovative composer. And as the evangelist? Consider his harmony an illumination of divine work. God gives the world a perfect phenomenon (in this case birdsong, but it could be, say, the gift of grace). To illumine a creation already perfect we use divinely given human powers. Here the divine gift is birdsong, and the human powers to illumine that gift are Messiaen's innate creativity leavened with his systemic rigor. Grace might be illumined by gifted preaching. Human powers are never required to understand God's gift because God gives understanding as well, but human powers can shed light on something to make clearer what God has created.

Rhythm. And now to time and rhythm, the nuclear core of Messiaen's music. Messiaen said in his lecture at the Brussels conference of 1958:

> Let us not forget that the first and most essential element in music is rhythm, and that rhythm is first and foremost the change of number and duration. Suppose that there were a single beat in all the universe. One beat: with eternity before it and eternity after it. A before and an after. That is the birth of time. Imagine then, almost immediately, a second beat. Since any beat is prolonged by the silence which follows it, the second beat will be longer than the first. Another number, another duration. That is the birth of rhythm.[18]

In *Oiseaux*, rhythm manifests itself in many ways. There are first the rhythms of the birdcalls, which make up a fast-moving and rhythmically spontaneous fabric. Shortly thereafter, the percussion instruments engage in a discourse of pointillistic transparency. These rhythms are based not on birdsongs or on standard Western rhythms (although in *Technique* chapters 3–7 he gives his ideas on manipulation of those rhythms in various configurations) but on another of Messiaen's passionate interests, Hindu rhythms from both northern (Hindustani) and especially southern (Karnatic) Indian tradition. He was attracted to Indian classical music not only for its rhythms but also its devotional quality. This respect for the devotion found in Hindu music, however, in no way undermined his belief in the primacy of the Christian God. "I have a great admiration for Hindu rhythms, but only for the rhythms — not

for Indian philosophy."[19]

In the appendix of his first treatise, and in his posthumous opus, *Treatise on Rhythm, Color and Birds,* Messiaen refers to the *Deci Talas* of Carngadeva, a thirteenth-century Hindu theorist. Messiaen renders one page of Carngadeva's work in chapter 4 of his *Treatise*, in which a fundamental rhythmic component of Indian classical music is described: namely, the *talas*. These are made up of long and short values, and they involve beats of durations both odd and even. Each is given a name unique to its rhythmic profile. While Western rhythmic motives are so often subservient to melody, gestural, and non-narrative, these Hindu rhythms are in themselves self-completing and often narrative, strung together cyclically, each tala being repeated a number of times until a clap or other signifying gesture is made. This gesture not only provides an opportunity to align the upper melodic and lower rhythmic elements, but can produce a new tala as well. Since talas often are not in the same rhythmic proportions as the simultaneous melodic material, they propel this music independent of the melodic stresses above them.

The Gajalila tala is present in *Oiseaux*. As the music progresses, the tala, clearly labeled on the score by Messiaen, is used in a way reminiscent of Indian music where two layers soar above the tala: the punctuating sixteenths in the instruments in the middle of the score, and the explosive melismatic figures above those (birdcalls).

Alongside these Hindu rhythms are the rhythms of Greek poetry. One can see how Messiaen would be attracted to these rhythmic forms: they are both poetic. He was a word-nurtured child, developing a love for the essential rhythms created by words perfectly set. Greek poetic rhythms are created by the length of words and syllables first, and by spoken word stresses second (although scholars disagree on the balance of these two factors). The numerous rhythms, based on "longum" and "breve," are each given specific names including (as those with Dalcroze training will quickly recognize) iambic, trochaic, dactylic, and anapestic.[20] Two examples, the asclepiadean and sapphic patterns, are faithfully rendered in *Oiseaux* by Messiaen.

Both the Indian and Greek rhythms are man-made rhetorical devices, the former musical, the latter linguistic. In their setting here does each represent a unique spiritual cultural concept revealed by the rhythms of rhetoric? Does one culture declaim clarity and focus while the other explores the un-tethered, the mystically obscure? In *Oiseaux* one notes two Greek-based rhythms and sees that these rhythms are focused in one instrumental timbre and provide a pulse-affirming rhythmic clarity, even when syncopated. As the rhythm of the Gajalila traverses the gong parts one finds a different idea. The Hindu rhythms here work to obscure beats, to plasticize the foundation, and to sound in one timbre. The Greek and Hindu rhythmic ideas exist in the same time frame, and exercise different intents, yet complement each other in serving a larger whole.

That larger whole is conceived from Messiaen's love and use of plainchant (see chapter 8 of *Technique*) and its abundant progeny, the motet. This love is evident in how these lines of rhythm work with the rest of the music traveling above. These rhythms act as a subtle cantus firmus as they support and inform the rigorous working out of the birdsong polyphony. Oiseaux lives much like an isorhythmic motet: a medieval/renaissance Western polyphonic texture built on a hierarchy of activity beginning with a long note value as a base, topped by a more active moderate level, topped yet again by one or two more levels of increasing activity, all somehow related to that essential base level.

Messiaen has in his use of these rhythms turned upside down the dominion hierarchy of nature and humankind, one with humankind at the top. The man-made rhetoric, Greek and Hindu in very simple realization, serves a foundational but subordinate role. Above the human

labors soars the elaborate and free fantasia of God's creation—birdsong—almost oblivious to the underlying efforts. Human rhetoric pales in comparison to the vivid rhetoric of God's most freely living creations.

The large form. We have explored the basic compositional elements of *Oiseaux*: birdsong, harmony, and rhythm. However, the most crucial issue to consider is the large form. Certainly performers need to track the basic elements making up a work, but that tracking can fall into mere accountancy if it is not in the service of discovering the large form and the musical trajectory through that form.

Oiseaux exotiques is constructed on two levels. The first level is one of "moment form," roughly defined as the form of a work made up of a string of events sequenced not necessarily for a progressive, organic narrative flow but for how each event is perceived singularly as it occurs. Stockhausen says of moment forms, "They are forms in a state of always having already commenced, which could go on as they are for an eternity."[21] And Jonathon Kramer says this about moment form in Messiaen: "Like Eastern music which deals with quality of mind, Messiaen's music does not ask to be followed as consistent, continuous thought. Instead, it creates conditions for mental excitation or reflection. If conventional Western music is narrative in its integrated, goal oriented planning, Messiaen's is by contrast liturgical: structured in self-contained blocks, proceeding by statement rather than development, by exposition rather than argument" (ibid., 283).

Many feel that the sequence of alternating sections of solo piano and ensemble parts in *Oiseaux* constitutes moment form and is sufficient to conclude a discussion of its large scale form. However, there is a larger view: closer inspection reveals the shadow of a form that goes far back in music history: the palindrome. There is a case to be made that the explosive beginning returns at the very end by way of a mirror image of the progression that leads from the beginning up to the middle. Hence that middle material is not only a climax, it is a turning point from which we return to our origin by an eerily similar path. Although by no means perfectly symmetrical, the pattern revealed is musically compelling, and even more compelling when considered evangelically. This palindrome reveals a musical diptych hinged in the middle, a picture of the human life cycle in which "all come from dust, and to dust all return" (Ecclesiastes 3:20). It is this large-scale form, this modern sonic counterpart to the sacred diptychs of medieval artists, that makes *Oiseaux* a singularly significant work.

Saint Francis of Assisi

Between 1975 and 1983 Messiaen engaged in a labor of ultimate synthesis: a bonding together of his intense belief, religious devotion, musical skill, and lifelong quest for his own *gesamtkunstwerk*. The result was *Saint Francis of Assisi*, his only opera (or "stage play" as he called it to invoke a descriptor less culturally-burdened).[22] It is no coincidence that the Umbrian saint became the chosen focus of Messiaen's final large, and arguably most representative, work.

Messiaen knew well the legend of Francis, who was born circa 1181 to Pietro and Pica Bernardone, and named Giovanni at his christening; his name was changed to Francis in childhood, possibly as a nod to his father's successful textile trade with the French, or to his mother's Provençal heritage. Francis indulged heartily in the life of a prodigal son, but did exhibit the virtue of charity, mainly by paying for his friends' shares of their earthly vices.[23] At about age twenty, after enlisting to fight the Perugians, he was captured and imprisoned. His awareness of spiritual issues was intensified about this time by two events that he experienced in captivity. The first was a bout of dangerous fever, which caused him to dramatically confront his mortality; this was followed by a dream that he was surrounded by armor emblazoned with crosses, in which he heard the words, "These are for you and your soldiers." This dream compelled him to pursue knighthood, to the medieval mind a wedding of military honor with spiritual piety (186).

The seed of faith had been planted and Francis was changing. His response to his mates' chiding regarding marriage was, "Yes, I am about to take of wife of surpassing fairness," a reference to his "Lady Poverty." In rather quick succession events drew Francis into a devoted, self-sacrificing life. His divinely inspired embrace of a leper was a first step towards a life of caring intimately for the infirm and destitute. His father, enraged by Francis's religious zeal, disinherited and abandoned him. Francis met rage with joy; he was now unburdened by earthly wealth. This series of revelations ended as Francis received divine commands to rescue chapels and churches from disrepair, his first in a lifetime of calls to action (187-99). Other men followed the charismatic friar, considered by most to be mad owing to his intense spiritual passion and hermit-like lifestyle. Collectively these followers became Francis's papally-sanctioned formal order: the Friars Minor. This is the origin of the Franciscan Order we know today, dedicated to charity, kindness, and evangelism through example, with adherents conscripted to the freeing joys of poverty.

Through twenty years of selfless toil Francis went on crusade to Spain and the Middle East, preached in piazzas, on church steps, in fields, and passionately devoted himself to Catholic dogma and leadership. Through the biography of Saint Francis written by his contemporary Friar Thomas of Celano, and the *Fioretti di Santo Francesco d' Assisi* (anecdotes from Francis's life written by others who knew him), a picture emerges of a divinely inspired man who lived in great contrast to the withdrawn, forbidding, and venally selfish clergy that populated the medieval Christian landscape. Francis was gregarious, charming in his eccentricities, and passionate to incorporate all of God's creatures into a church that included the whole of a God-made creation.

Messiaen and Saint Francis. How did these two gifted men respond to their manifold personal gifts, gifts that made them both world-renowned?[24] Both men were exceedingly humble in harvesting the fruits of their gifts. Messiaen had an extraordinary reputation for humility, and Saint Francis's gestures of humility are extensively chronicled. Both men lived out humility in their daily labors: Messiaen continued as a parish church musician after worldwide fame was his, and Francis served the destitute until his death.

Along with humility, Saint Francis and Messiaen shared a similar, seminal life experience: a loss of freedom through imprisonment in young adulthood. Freedom is a complex idea in Christian theology. Freedom without God—human freedom—is quite often a curse, an opportunity to ignore or squander the deeply important gifts of life. It often brings solitude rather than companionship, wealth but not fulfillment. In his wartime loss of human freedom, clearly Messiaen was divinely inspired to compose his extraordinarily clear and passionate synthesis of art and faith. Francis's imprisonment made him an immobile target for the divine spark; his loss of human freedom was replaced by a freedom in God's care.

What links Francis and Messiaen? Most obvious is the role of birds in the lives of both men.

For Francis, the words of Christ (Matthew 6:26) regarding poverty and birds must have been both reassuring and liberating. The birds do not starve, says Jesus, because the Father takes care of them; so will he then take care of the friars of the Order. These creatures enjoy a surpassing freedom to simply live, and to live simply, because of their reliance on God. The following part of the Franciscan legend would forever make inseparable Saint Francis and birds:

> Saint Francis lifted up his eyes, and saw
> on some trees by the wayside a great
> multitude of birds…and the substance of

the sermon [to them] was this: "My little sisters the birds, ye owe much to God, your Creator, and ye ought to sing his praise at all times and in all places, because he has given you liberty to fly about into all places; and though ye neither spin nor sew, he has given you a twofold and a three-fold clothing for yourselves and for your offspring; besides which, he feeds you, though ye neither sow nor reap. He has given you fountains and rivers to quench your thirst, mountains and valleys in which to take refuge, and trees in which to build your nests; so that your Creator loves you much, having thus favoured you with such bounties. Beware, my little sisters, of the sin of ingratitude, and study always to give praise to God." As he said these words, all the birds began to open their beaks, to stretch their necks, to spread their wings and reverently to bow their heads to the ground, endeavouring by their motions and by their songs to manifest their joy to Saint Francis. And the saint rejoiced with them (234).

The legendary tale of the birds makes up act 2, scene 6 in Messiaen's opera. In the opening of the scene one can hear the birds of Messiaen's 1956 *Oiseaux exotique* brought together again for *Saint Francis* in 1983. Francis and his brother Masseo discuss the meaning of the birds. Does the meaning of the birds to Francis have bearing on Messiaen?

Birds, unencumbered by human or sectarian strife, praise in easy and immediate response to the gifts of life from God. In a panel discussion of June 1972, Messiaen said this: "I don't belong to any kind of school; I'm neither a follower of serial music, nor am I a composer of a 'new sound,' nor do I champion the cause of any special modes."[25] Messiaen thus defines his freedom to praise, his non-sectarian position among composers. Messiaen is indeed sectarian in his unwavering belief in the Creed and

Catholicism: his works offered "at the service of the dogmas of the Catholic faith" are "the only [works] perhaps I will not regret at the hour of my death."[26] However, in his use of God-given compositional gifts, his sectarian impulse gives way to a freeing, universal Christian praise, as free and universal as birdsong.

The metaphor and reality of birdsong extend further. As Messiaen chose not to define himself by a school of composition, Francis chose not to encourage narrow schools of thought or structured theology in proclaiming his Gospel message. Rather, he communicated ideas directly from Scripture as they passed through his heart. Francis and Messiaen were compelled to proclaim messages that were straightforward. (A new listener to Messiaen might mistake the novelty, and the busy-ness, of his music for complexity. We have seen how the music is in reality a synthesis of many simple elements of nature.) Messiaen felt he composed as Francis preached: "in words few and chaste," just as birdsong is art pure and simple.[27]

Finally, there is something shared between these two men that may transcend all: a belief that their works would be accepted and embraced by non-believers, and the seeds of their belief would be planted in new ground. Messiaen advocated that his music be performed in many venues, not exclusively, or even primarily, in churches. He emphasized that "God is present everywhere," and so he felt that his musical message should be heard over a wide world.[28] Francis, by preaching at every crossroads and piazza, ensured that all would hear the Word.

Mysticism. Despite their similarities there is an important way in which these two men differed, and that has to do with their perspectives on mysticism. Messiaen's music is often described as mystical. When asked whether he considered himself a mystic he replied:

> Personally, I deeply distrust the word. It doesn't suit me at all and I'd like to say why

not. As soon as one starts talking about mysticism, people think of a diseased state, of a neurotic who has vague sentiments and ecstasies. I don't like that, I am a devout man and I love the sound, solid gifts of faith. There were real mystics with real visions and ecstasies … such things existed. But no one is a mystic of his own will …[29]

Francis, on the other hand, was a true mystic. His experiences with the Holy Spirit, including receiving the stigmata, connected him to the real God and dictated his actions here on earth. Comparison of the two men highlights how the lack of mystical experience seemed to lead Messiaen to attempt to transcend earthly bounds, to lead us a few rungs closer to the Divine. Francis truly encountered the mystical, and was compelled to get closer and closer to earth in order to manifest the mystical revelation. Messiaen painted for us the celestial city without actually seeing it, and Francis, having encountered it, attempted to recreate its beneficent face on earth.

And then, finally, what of our directive for this Colloquium? Have we today tackled "inculturation"? Messiaen and Francis both serve as examples of broadly directed evangelism. Current thinking increasingly insists that cultures embrace their identity. This search for cultural self often, one hopes unintentionally, actually inspires cultural division. Francis and Messiaen ignore division of cultures and instead bring them together. By mixing global birdsong with Indian and Greek voices, medieval European and contemporary classical musical styles, Messiaen elevates all elements by equating all elements in the process. Francis did the same: all strata, all God's creation, with joyous disregard for rank and wealth, can contribute to the richness of Christian devotion. By never elevating one singly, the sum is raised up. How marvelous for us that God joined together these two humble, imaginative, zealous evangelists to proclaim His creation.

ENDNOTES

1. "Olivier Messiaen: Address Delivered at the Confer-ring of the Praemium Erasmianum on June 25, 1971 in Amsterdam," in *Contributions to the Spiritual World of Olivier Messiaen: with Original Texts by the Composer*, ed. Almut Roessler (Duisberg: Gilles and Francke, 1986), 39.

2. Carla Huston Bell, *Olivier Messiaen* (Boston: Twayne, 1984), 11.

3. Claude Samuel, "Conversation 1," in *Conversations with Olivier Messiaen*, trans. Felix Aprahamian (Lon-don: Stainer and Bell, 1976), 18.

4. Peter Hill and Nigel Simeone, "Childhood and the Conservatoire: 1908-1929," in *Messiaen* (New Haven: Yale University Press, 2005), 9-24.

5. Idem, "Messiaen's War: 1940-1944," in *Messiaen*, 99-100.

6. Claude Samuel, "Conversation 7," in *Conversations with Olivier Messiaen*, 115.

7. Bell, *Olivier Messiaen*, 1.

8. See Olivier Messiaen, *Music and Color: Conversa-tions with Claude Samuel*, trans. E. Thomas Glasgow (Portland: Amadeus Press, 1994), 13-14.

9. Olivier Messiaen, *The Technique of My Musical Lan-guage*, trans. John Satterfield (Paris: Alphonse Leduc, 1956), 7.

10. "Encounters with Olivier Messiaen," in *Contribu-tions*, ed. Roessler, 33.

11. Matthew Gurewitsch, "Messiaen: An Audubon in Sound," *The Atlantic Monthly* 279/3 (1997), online edition.

12. "Encounters with Olivier Messiaen," in *Contribu-tions*, ed. Roessler, 32.

13. "Natural Harmony," in *The Technique*, 52.

14. Robert Sherlaw Johnson, "The Development of Messiaen's Musical Language," in *Messiaen* (Berkeley: University of California Press, 1975), 16.

15. "Conversation with Olivier Messiaen on December 16, 1983, in Paris," in *Contributions*, ed. Roessler, 122.

16. Bell, *Olivier Messiaen*, 30.

17. Johnson, *Messiaen* ,19.

18. Bell, *Olivier Messiaen*, 5.

19. "Conversation with Olivier Messiaen on April 23, 1979, in Paris," in *Contributions*, ed. Roessler, 97.

20. James W. Halporn, et al., *The Meters of Greek and Latin Poetry* (Indianapolis: Bobbs-Merrill, 1963).

21. Jonathan D. Kramer, *The Time of Music: New Mean-ings, New Temporalities, New Listening Strategies* (New York: Schirmer Books, 1988), 201.

22. "Conversation with Olivier Messiaen on December 16, 1988, in Paris," in *Contributions*, ed. Roessler, 119.

23. Regis Armstrong et al., eds., "The Life of Saint Francis of Assisi by Thomas Celano: The First Book," in *Francis of Assisi: Early Documents* (New York: New City Press, 1999), 183-84.

24. Thomas Celano observed that "I saw a great multitude of people coming at us…. I seemed to see highways filled with this multitude … from every na-tion …" (ibid., 206).

25. "Platform Discussion on June 11, 1972, in the Bach Hall of Saint John's Church," in *Contributions*, ed. Roessler, 54.

26. Madeleine Hsu [Forte], "Messiaen in His Time," in *Olivier Messiaen, the Musical Mediator* (Cranbury: Associated University Presses, 1996), 25.

27. Regis Armstrong et al., eds., "The Later Rule," in *Francis of Assisi: Early Documents* (New York: New City Press, 1999), 105.

28. Messiaen, *Music and Color*, 147.

29. "Conversation with Olivier Messiaen on April 23, 1979, in Paris," in *Contributions*, ed. Roessler, 89.

ADDITIONAL READING

Bruhn, Siglind, ed. *Messiaen's Language of Mystical Love*. New York: Garland, 1998.

Englebrecht, Omar. *Saint Francis of Assisi: A Biography*. Ann Arbor: Servant Books, 1979.

Galli, Mark. *Francis of Assisi and His World*. London: Lion Publishing, 2002.

Green, Julien. *God's Fool: The Life and Times of Francis of Assisi*. San Francisco: Harper and Row, 1983.

Griffiths, Paul. *Olivier Messiaen and the Music of Time*. Ithaca: Cornell University Press, 1985.

Holcomb, Paula K. *Oiseaux Exotique: A Conductor's*

Score Study Guide. DMA diss., Northwestern University, 1992.

Messiaen, Olivier. *Conférence de Notre-Dame: prononcée à Notre-Dame de Paris le 4 décember 1977.* Paris: Alphonse Leduc, 1978.

Messiaen, Olivier. *Conférence de Bruxelles en 1958.* Paris: Alphonse Leduc, 1960.

Messiaen, Olivier. *Traité de rythme, de couleur, et d'ornithologie.* 7 vols. Paris: Alphonse Leduc, 1994.

Sabatier, Paul. *The Essential Biography of Saint Francis,* annotated by John Sweeney. Brewster, Mass.: Paraclete Press, 2003.

Charles Peltz is on the faculty of the New England Conservatory where he directs the wind ensemble and teaches graduate conducting. He is the music director of the Glens Falls Symphony Orchestra, a professional orchestra in upstate New York, and is a regular guest conductor of the Orquesta Nacional de Colombia in Bogotá. He records for MODE records.

ISM Student Presentations

Dance and Its Use in the Chorale Cantatas of J. S. Bach

RICHARD GARD

Richard Gard received the Director's Prize for best student Colloquium presentation in 2004.
His presentation is included in almost complete form on the accompanying DVD.

It is well known that Johann Sebastian Bach utilized dance forms in his compositions. But Bach incorporated a variety of styles, genres, and textures in his music—could it be that dance was just one more resource in his compositional palette?

Owing to the pervasive notoriety and social importance of dance, it is likely that dance forms and textures conveyed an embedded message for Bach and for his audience that would make their inclusion in sacred music notable. Furthermore, acknowledging dance as a social ritual raises interesting questions about the practice of inserting secular music and dramatic forms into liturgical services. Many seventeenth- and eighteenth-century German pastors and musicians had no qualms about the wholesale importation and mixing of operatic recitative and aria, folk tunes and medieval melodies—or even a jolly dance—in their worship music. This intersection of sacred and secular offers a lesson of diversity and inclusion for twenty-first-century musicians and liturgists.

This talk will show that during the years 1723 and 1724 Bach experimented with a compositional technique using a noble dance (usually the sarabande) in the penultimate movement of some chorale cantatas. The technique was refined during his second Leipzig cycle and continued for as long as he composed chorale cantatas; it was used in connection with images of heaven, Advent, and Jesus as the bridegroom.

Richard Gard enjoys a successful career as a conductor and educator. He conducts several performance ensembles including the Yale Bruckner Choir, the NVCC College Choir, the Western Connecticut State University Concert Choir, Vox Concordis, the Richard Gard Singers, and the Wind Ensemble of Western Connecticut. He is the director of music at Saint Thomas More Chapel at Yale. He is also chair at Naugatuck Valley Community College, Connecticut's most comprehensive two-year music program. He will receive his DMA in May of 2007. Richard continues to apply the fruits of his dance research with recent performances of Bach's Cantata 80 *and Handel's* Chandos Anthem 6.

.

ISM Colloquium Presentation Abstracts

Spring 2005

Callista Brown Isabelle
Shape Note Singing: Music of the New Frontier

Shape note singing, developed in singing schools in the 1720s, was a vibrant musical form in colonial America. In my presentation we explored its history and sang the shape note version of *Wondrous Love*, and I argued that this music may enrich our liturgies even today. Ways of incorporating shape note singing into the musical life of your congregation include organ/piano improvisations on the shape note tunes, holding shape note singings in your church or community, performing choir anthems, etc. This music can deepen congregants' understanding of early American Christianity, build bridges in our struggles over traditional vs. contemporary, aid in music literacy and congregational singing, and offer a message of radical "welcome" through shared leadership and full congregational participation.

1. How might shape note singing supplement the liturgical practices of your congregation?
2. What are the limitations of shape note singing for use in worship today?
3. What are the "new frontiers" of sacred music and/or liturgy today?

Mina Choi
The Plainsong Restoration in Nineteenth and Twentieth Century French Organ Music

The nineteenth century French organist Alexandre Guilmant (1837-1911) summarized his view of liturgical organ music late in his career as the following: "The German organists have composed some pieces based on the melody of cho-rales, forming a literature for the organ which is particularly rich; why should we not do the same with our Catholic melodies?" Plainsong restoration in France influenced organ music in the late nineteenth and the twentieth centuries toward the development of a truly contemporary style of liturgical organ music based on an intimate knowledge and appreciation of plainsong, and the technique of the modern French symphonic style of organ music. Organist-composers like Widor, Guilmant, and Tournemire expanded the idea of sacred idealism by displaying liturgical melodies and texts in a new type of liturgical organ music.

1. How important is knowledge of the plainsong texts in modern liturgical organ music based on plainsong?
2. How might plainsong-based liturgical music (organ versets) be used in the Protestant church?
3. Do you gain an idea of sacred idealism just by hearing repetitive chant tunes in the symphonic genre?

Kimberly Dunn
Francis Poulenc's Litanies à la Vierge Noir: *A Spiritual Awakening*

Francis Poulenc's work for women's choir and organ, *Litanies à la Vierge Noire, Notre-Dame de Roc-Amadour*, is more than a sublime piece of music. As the first of an important series of sacred choral pieces, it occupies a significant place within Poulenc's compositional output. The true value of this work can only be understood through an in-depth analysis of the historical, thematic, biographical, religious, and musical factors influencing its birth.

The circumstances surrounding Poulenc's return to Catholicism are widely noted in biographical sources, and the death of a close friend in a car accident is considered the turning point in Poulenc's spiritual life. His subsequent pilgrimage to the cathedral at Roc-Amadour, home of the *Vierge Noire* or "Throne of Wisdom," solidified his commitment to the Catholic faith, and resulted in the creation of the *Litanies*. An acquaintance with the history of the cathedral and the legends of the Virgin transforms the text of this piece—a series of petitions to the benevolent and miraculous Virgin—from a series of requests into fervent pleas alternating between spiritual meditation and ecstasy.

By recognizing the spiritual intensity of this juncture in Poulenc's life, one can interpret and perform the musical elements of this piece more effectively. Musical analysis, contextualized by non-musical analysis, also has greater meaning. The sectional form and cyclical structure of the piece serve the text, while the dissonant "shock" chords evoke emotional turmoil. Melodic devices such as additive phrasing create a meditative atmosphere, while faux bourdon provokes a strong sense of movement. These musical devices all shape the emotional ambiance of the composition, and indeed are understood more deeply when placed within the space and circumstance for which they were written. While we do not have to believe in the religious and emotional foundations of the *Litanies*, it is important that we be aware of all musical and non-musical elements in order to fully experience the composition.

1.   Do you feel that it is important as a director, performer, or listener to be aware of the non-musical history and context of the piece? How would this information shape (or not shape) your interpretation, presentation, and perception of the music?
2.   How do musical devices such as additive phrasing, ecclesiastical modes, and faux bourdon evoke a mood and shape the emo-

tional/spiritual orientation of the composition?
3.   How might this piece be used in worship? Does the text lend itself to an inclusive and communal expression of faith?

Erik Eickhoff
"Do You Hear What I Hear?"—Performer's Intention and Listener's Interpretation

While examining a piece of contemporary music, and what Karl Barth said of Mozart, I asked what the relationship between a composer's (or performer's) intention and a listener's interpretation is. Music is first aesthetic and then communicative. Music is powerful — but power is not a substitute for clarity. We cannot know a composer's communicative intention by simply examining his or her music. Because the intention does not lead to a necessary interpretation, the composer is, in a sense, dead; it is the music that speaks, not the composer.

1.   In the case of a contemporary piece, can we know the composer's intention?
2.   What does it mean to say that music is first aesthetic and then communicative? Does this mean, for example, that beauty does not tell us anything?
3.   What does it mean to say that music is powerful?
4.   If an intention does not lead to a necessary interpretation, then what are the implications for biblical hermeneutics?
5.   The abstract says that music is not first communicative and yet music speaks. Is this not a contradiction?

Victoria Gardner
The Secret of the Rosary

I attempted to unveil the mystery of the Rosary for those with little or no knowledge of it, first outlining its history, and then discussing the natural development of the use of beads as prayer counters, citing examples of this from all major religions. I also discussed how the Rosary prayers changed from Our Fathers to Hail Marys owing to an increased devotion to Mary in the Middle Ages and the development of "Mary Psalters." Second, I explained the purpose of the Rosary, both in its original and its contemporary form, describing how it developed from being a shortcut for the Divine Office to becoming a way to meditate on the life and work of Christ. Third, I described how the Rosary is prayed both individually and communally by giving a detailed description of the mechanics of praying the Rosary. Finally, I discussed how the Rosary can be used in modern times by all people and churches. J. Neville Ward, a Methodist, and Pope John Paul II both considered the Rosary an aid to ecumenism. I ended my presentation with an exhortation to the audience to use the Rosary prayer, a traditional Christan way of meditation, for spiritual sustenance, rather than seeking spirituality in other religions and other ways.

1. How might people who are prejudiced against anything Marian feel comfortable praying the Rosary? Prejudices often come from a lack of information or from misinformation. One should become educated about Mary, and also about the scriptural and theological basis of the "Hail Mary" prayer, and realize that Mary plays an essential role in salvation history and therefore it is very Christian to honor her (even Luther recognized this!).

2. How might a non-Catholic use the Rosary prayer in a congregation? The same way a Catholic would! Catholics often get together in groups to pray it before or after a church service. Anyone can start it at any time, and then everyone joins in. Catholics also pray the Rosary by themselves, whenever they wish to. It can be prayed anywhere—in a church, a car, the shower—so that one can

think of the Scriptures all the time. It's so easy! Even children can learn their Scripture through the Rosary.

Brian Harlow
"The Spacious Firmament on High": The Integration of English Hymnody into Noye's Fludde *by Benjamin Britten*

The presentation focused on Britten's use of hymns in *Noye's Fludde*. These hymn settings are significant for two reasons: first, they are scored for the entire assembly; and second, they are connected to the overall musical texture and structure of the work in a number of ways. Britten blurs the conventional boundaries between performer and audience/congregation, and between concert and worship. The change in relationship between the audience and the composition arguably creates better listeners. Britten also blends Western hymnody and twentieth century art music with sounds from Eastern cultures. Bringing together the many musical elements, as well as the audience and performers, reinforces the universal ideal presented in Joseph Addison's hymn "The Spacious Firmament on High."

1. Do you feel that participating in the performance of music such as *Noye's Fludde* would enhance your ability to listen to the rest of the piece?

2. Would you sing the hymns along with the audience if there were things in the text with which you did not agree? In other words, would you consider your role as a personal expression of faith (worship) or as part of the performance?

3. Do you feel that Britten's combination of musical styles and elements is successful or contrived?

Lindsey Henriksen

"But Now We Know Better . . .": How an Organ Can Shape the Sonic Landscape of a Church

In this presentation I investigated the way that a particular kind of organ can shape the musical sonic landscape of a congregation. Twentieth- and twenty-first-century organ builders and scholars have spent a lot of time considering not only the history of the organ's repertoire but also the history of the instrument. Now that we "know better" about the history of organ con-struction, has this knowledge shaped the music in our churches? How do our organs reflect and respond to the needs of our congregations? How do the instruments themselves shape the music in our churches?

Next I gave a short history of organ design and construction beginning with the early mod-ern organ of 1450 and ending with the artisan organ building trend of the twenty-first century. In order to find out how these principles of or-gan design influenced real, practicing musicians in New Haven I posed a series of questions to local area organists. The questions were:

What is the general makeup of your congrega-tion?

Do you have a regular choir?

What kind of education does the organist have?

Tell me about the organ and its background.

What style is it? Was it installed before or after you became the organist?

How is the organ used during worship? What kind of repertoire is played?

What isn't played because of the organ's restric-tions?

What types of music other than organ music are used?

How important is the organ in the music of your church?

Do you feel that the organ's style matches the needs of your congregation?

How would you change the organ to make it more effective?

How does the organ work in the church as a functional piece of art (like an altar or pulpit)?

How would the worship service change if you had only a piano?

What do you see for the future of the organ in your church?

I concluded that the best organ-church relationships occur when the organist takes an active role in promoting the strengths of the organ, and the clergy/worship leaders carefully investigate the strengths and weaknesses of the instrument in their church.

1. What are some good ways to introduce a church's organ to those who may be unfa-miliar with it?
2. What is the future of the organ in church worship? Why?

Rick Hoffenberg

An Artistic Amalgamation: Kierkegaard's Words and Barber's Music

Samuel Barber, an American, became the only major composer to set texts of the Danish theo-logian and philosopher Søren Kierkegaard when he wrote his cantata, *Prayers of Kierkegaard,* in 1954. The piece reveals a wide variety of musical influences, including Gregorian chant, German baroque cantatas, and twelve-tone methods. Barber utilized a variety of means on both a small and large scale to depict and enhance Kierkegaard's words. Choices of melody, har-mony, rhythm, dynamics, and instrumentation can often be traced directly to the meaning of the words. Barber also explored different effects of the same phrase, as with the frenzied, almost shouted setting of "Father in Heaven," followed by an extremely hushed rendering of these same words. On a broader level, the progression of key areas at important structural points correlates to shifts in the tone of Kierkegaard's writing.

1. Taken alone, the texts Barber selected give a distorted and overly simplistic view of Kierkegaard's thoughts. Is it a mark against Barber that he did not try to deal with the Kierkegaard of, for example, *Either/Or*, *Fear and Trembling*, and *Concluding Unscientific Postscript*?

2. I proposed that Barber arranged Kierkegaard's texts in reverse chronological order so that a pattern of increasing confidence and optimism would pervade the piece, underscored by Barber's choice of keys. For what other reasons might a composer manipulate the order of texts in fashioning a large-scale piece?

3. What level of responsibility does a composer bear in accurately and appropriately setting the words of an author? Should a composer be free to set a text in any way he/she chooses?

Cecelia Jones
Praise and Worship: The Sound of Heaven

I showed how the Praise and Worship liturgy happens in many congregations. While this orginated in Charismatic/Pentecostal traditions it can be found in many mainline churches as a liturgical movement, and is filled with pneumological and eschatological theology. Secondly, I discussed the essence of the worship leader in a Praise and Worship service, particularly focusing on the spiritual component to his/her leadership. The Worship Institute, an itinerant ministry in Dallas, Texas, was briefly compared to the ISM as a place that fosters musical and spiritual readiness for parish ministry.

1. How exactly are Praise and Worship liturgies different from other congregational sung-worship experiences?

2. What makes this liturgy so effective?

3. How does culture play into this liturgy?

Erika Jones
The Manifestation of Dance in the African American Worship Service

[Abstract not available]

Woo-sug Kang
Herbert Howells and His Psalm Preludes

Herbert Howells, a twentieth-century Anglican composer, is well known for his sacred choral music. Many pieces besides the choral works, however, are of high quality, and valuable for church musicians. His first set of psalm preludes for organ was written at a time when he was mainly writing secular pieces; they are in an improvisational style, and show his unique harmonic language and introspective approach to the text and music. His ability to express his personal ideas about the meaning of the text through his music allows him to create his own personal sounds. This way of setting the mood of the psalm text helps listeners to receive the music and interpret it within their own personal contexts.

1. How can we use the psalm preludes in non-Anglican church services?

2. To what extent do Howells's psalm preludes comment upon or interpret the psalm text?

3. How important is knowing and understanding the text in listening to this music?

Betsy Moss
Where Are the Artists?

In this presentation I examine the work of several artists and several aspects of art production. These include (1) redefining "spiritual" as that which emerges from within our religious communities; (2) understanding viewers of artworks as participants instead of spectators; and (3) developing new art-making techniques (such as Shantz's breaking twigs). It is my aim to develop a deeper relationship between our churches and the artworld—not to reform one for the other's purposes.

1. Do you think it possible for our society to have spiritual/religious art that locates the spiritual not in the mysterious outsider but in ourselves joined together as a community?
2. Is education, or experience with an art form, the best way to grant access to this art form? What do you think of participation in an art form as a way to enrich our lives together?
3. Imagine you are an artist: do you think your work as an artist can change people or communities? Do you feel responsible to your audience/community? Do you expect anything from your audience? If so, is the work you are making still art?

Kristin Naragon
The Experience of Meaning in Music: Perspectives from the Social Sciences

We now understand a person's prior experience with music, both at the cultural and individual level, to be an important factor in how that person generates meaning in music. There are two primary views of how musical meaning is created: Kivy's "Cognitivism" claims that music cannot express emotions, but is expressive of emotions through resemblance to emotive life. Narmour's Implication-Realization Model posits that the listener perceives emotions in music when the music does not fulfill the listener's moment-by-moment expectations for the music, thus creating a pattern of tension and relaxation. Empirical research shows that people can reliably identify basic emotions in music, and can understand the basic features of an unfamiliar musical system without extensive training, but that they have difficulty understanding the emotional meaning of the music as a native listener would. There is a strong relationship between

liking a style of music and prior experience with it, as people tend to like music with a moderate subjective complexity. Applied to worship, these findings suggest that it is important to provide congregations with some familiar music, but also that new music can be introduced successfully without extensive training. Finally, it shows that musical meaning can be sucessfully communicated in a limited but real sense.

1. Do the theories of musical meaning presented (Kivy and Narmour) seem accurate in your experience with music? What are their respective strengths and weaknesses?
2. How important is prior experience with music in our understanding of its meaning?
3. What are some practical implications for how we can best incorporate unfamiliar music into worship services?

William Ng
Dead Serious: Reading Chinese-Christian Tombstones in Hong Kong, a Case Study of Inculturation

The tightly-knit traditional Chinese family structure is the hallmark of Confucian ideology, forming the backbone of Chinese culture and society. Filial piety is the prime virtue; it transcends life and death, and is celebrated by an ancestral cult. Graves are its visible expression. The ancestral cult consists of a twice-a-year "grave sweeping" ritual. An auspicious location is chosen for the graves by feng-shui principles in order to bring prosperity to the descendants. The traditional shape of a grave is the half-moon.

During the Rites Controversy in eighteenth-century China one of the two issues was whether ancestral rituals are religious worship or cultural ceremonies. At that time they were suppressed, but in 1939 Rome decided that these rites had been desacralized and so ancestral devotion was permitted finally. Even to this day, however, most Protestants still see ancestral devotion as an impediment to evangelization.

A case study of two Christian cemeteries in Hong Kong shows various examples of positive/negative inculturation. "Positive inculturation" includes recognizing the place of women in society, and a creative adoption of Chinese elements. "Negative inculturation" includes using a non-Chinese way of incorporating baptismal names, tolerance of concubinage, excluding names of daughters and granddaughters on the graves, and prohibition of any external rituals and of a particular design for graves.

1. Is it really possible to Christianize ancestral cults/ancestral devotions/ancestral rites? Why?
2. How can Chinese Christians in Hong Kong express their dual identities as Chinese and Christian through the visual culture (graves, rites, buildings, etc.)? Who makes the decision?
3. Possibly not many of us will become missionaries, but do we face any conflicts between culture and faith?

Christiana Peppard
The Stuff of Life and the Place of the Dead

This presentation explored the significance of a columbarium that was recently installed at the Episcopal Church of St. Paul and St. James in New Haven. Part I of the presentation was an historical timeline of the use of columbaria, emphasizing especially their origin (during the time of Caesar Augustus) and the recent history and form of columbaria in America. Part II consisted of an explication of the design and function of the columbarium recently installed inside Sts. P&J. This columbarium bisects the vertical axis of the worship space so that a person entering the front doors of the church will pass by the baptismal font, through the columbarium, then through the central aisle and pews, and up to the altar. Theological considerations, liturgical changes, and possible benefits and drawbacks of

the design and placement of the columbarium were discussed. Part III raised the question of whether (and how) the columbarium might reflect the theological and ethical life of the congregation. In particular, historical and contemporary socioeconomic arguments about cremation were juxtaposed with evidence of Sts. P&J's emphasis on social justice.

1. In your estimation, what is (or ought to be) the relationship between "the stuff of life" (such as worship, celebration, or other active congregational life) and "the place of the dead"?
2. What effects, good or bad, might a columbarium such as the one at Sts. P&J have for the life of the community? For the life of the liturgy?
3. Do you find the ethical arguments about socioeconomic status and burial practice to be compelling? What are the benefits and drawbacks of burial vs. cremation?
4. In general, do you think that there is a relationship among the design of the worship space, the liturgy, and the ethical practices of a congregation? Why or why not?

Josh Probert
Remembering Brother Joseph: Iconography of Joseph Smith in LDS Worship Spaces.

Mormonism was born in a Protestant environment that largely avoided imagery in liturgical spaces, but, unlike their neighbors, Mormons became quite comfortable with iconography. This can be attributed to Brigham Young's encouragement of iconography combined with large populations of converts from Scandinavia and the British Isles—Christian centers comfortable with iconography. The subjects of Mormon iconography included scenes from the life of Jesus and the apostles, portraiture, images of temples, symbols borrowed from Freemasonry, and Mormon saints in the Latter-day sense of the word.

The first Latter-day saint, Joseph Smith, became a popular subject of Mormon iconography in the second half of the nineteenth century. His foundational experiences — the First Vision and deliverance of the golden plates — constitute the *muthos* of Mormonism. As visual canon, these stories served Mormons living in the intermountain West in the same way that the foundational stories of the Hebrew Bible served ancient Israel: they answered the questions required of canon, "Who are we?" and "What are we to do?"

1. How does history shape the contemporary identity of a religious community?
2. How does a culturally bound new religion create iconographic, musical, and liturgical novelty?

Michael Smith
Death and the Musician

Our society is faced with an inability to deal with death as death, and resurrection as resurrection. Instead, we substitute weak metaphors in our conversation and in our funeral rites. Using the examples of three choral works, I believe a new model for art dealing with these topics can be developed. Their synthesis of pre-existing texts and compositional techniques reveal hopeful theology concerning death and resurrection. As scholars and practitioners, we have a responsibility to commission, create, or otherwise locate art that fills this need for our communities.

1. What is the balance between recognizing the reality of death and offering comfort and solace?
2. How can worshipping communities better incorporate rites of death and dying into their common life?

Timothy Spelbring
The Orgelbüchlein: A View into the Genesis of Bach's Compositional Process

The chorale prelude played an elemental role in Bach's compositional output. His *Orgelbüchlein* (Little Organ Book) is perhaps the most influential collection of chorale preludes intended for use during the liturgical year. In examining the autograph score of this work, still extant today, one can gain an understanding of the compositional process Bach employed and the stages he worked through to arrive at the completed composition. Beyond technical matters, however, is the question of why this music was composed. What are the theological or emotive underpinnings behind the composition? Bach was not trained as a theologian, though his immersion in eighteenth-century ecclesiastical life certainly helped him gain theological insight. We considered a Passiontide chorale in the collection based on the German tune *O Mensch bewein dein Sünde gross* to help answer this question, and to give a bird's-eye view into the compositional process.

1. Do you feel it important to read the chorale text before listening to a chorale prelude? How might reading the text be helpful to you?
2. How might the *O Mensch bewein* chorale prelude be used in a corporate worship service? Keep in mind that chorales are rarely sung in American churches today.
3. Do you find the chorale prelude genre a useful method for introducing a chorale tune? In your experience, has the use of a chorale prelude helped to introduce the chorale tune, or prevented you from recognizing the tune?

Gilbert Sunghera, S.J.
How Do You Bury Arnold Schwarzenegger? Building a Cathedral in Contemporary Times.

The newly constructed Roman Catholic cathedral for Los Angeles exemplifies the many challenges faced when designing cathedrals in modern American cities. In the presentation, protestors were shown raising issues. The need was for a large civic/sacred space that addressed the diverse socioeconomic needs of the diocese and the city. Large spaces come at a heavy cost ($195 million). Modern liturgical reforms require changes to sacred spaces such as large cathedral settings — for example, minimized separation between sanctuary and nave, side chapels facing the ambulatory and not the nave, the tabernacle located in a separate chapel of reserve, etc. Grand cathedral spaces typically feature long mid-range reverberation rates—here designers reduced the reverberation rate to 3.5 seconds to accommodate both spoken and sung words (often of different languages). Finally, modern artists were upset with the quality of the art produced for the cathedral.

Rafael Moneo, the architect, along with Cardinal Mahoney and the building team, were able to create a cathedral in a modern architectural vocabulary. Many have said that it captures a sense of older cathedrals while being accessible to a modern and diverse population. In doing so, they created a successful cathedral for modern times, a proper place to bury Governor Arnold Schwarzenegger. However, were the issues raised by the protesters fully addressed?

1. General: The first civic funeral held at the cathedral was for a non-Catholic police officer, killed in the line of duty. Can civic/sacred space be created in the pluralistic reality of modern American cities, and at what financial cost?
2. Liturgist: What is the role of a cathedral in contemporary Catholic culture? Should it be built in line with the current reforms of liturgical practice even if this means significant changes to people's familiar experience of the sacred?
3. Musicians: Should a cathedral respond to the current music practices of local communities even if this means electronic amplification to achieve full and active participation? [Note: in the presentation three styles of music were featured: praise style from Arnold's church in Santa Monica; a fourteenth-century Spanish piece from Latin America using rhythm instruments; and a contemporary bilingual—English/Vietnamese—hymn. Can a new "cathedral sound" emerge in such diversity?]
4. Artists: What is the role of modern artists when enhancing houses of worship? [Two artistic pieces were presented: tapestries using photo-realist imagery, and the grand doors using sacred/non-Christian symbols.]

Fred Teardo
The Practice of Organ Improvisation in 19th/20th Century Paris: Liturgical Influences

Organ improvisation in *fin-de-siècle* Paris was very heavily influenced by aspects of the Catholic liturgy, most importantly plainchant and its revival in the nineteenth century. Other influences included the sound of the new symphonic organs being built by Aristide Cavaillé-Coll, and the emphasis on organ improvisation outside of church—from formal training at the Paris Conservatory to the secular concert stage. Two figures in the early twentieth century who were truly pivotal in the art form of organ improvisation were Charles Tournemire and Marcel Dupré. Tournemire was best known as an improviser. In 1930 he recorded five improvisations, including the famous *Improvisation sur le "Te Deum,"* later reconstructed by Maurice Duruflé. Tournemire's *L'Orgue mystique* attempts to capture the improvised Mass in written form for fifty-one Sundays of the liturgical year. Marcel

Dupré stretched the limits of liturgy's influences on improvisation by improvising a full-scale organ symphony based on submitted plainchant themes in the Wanamaker Department Store in Philadelphia, perhaps the most secular of arenas. Both Tournemire and Dupré wrote methods for learning improvisation that employ plainchant extensively as a model for improvisation on a theme. The art of improvisation in Paris is still very much alive, and provides an example of an art form that all of us may incorporate into our worship.

1. Though improvisation in Paris is very much rooted in the Catholic liturgy, how might we go about incorporating such a model of improvisation in our own worship?
2. How can today's congregations benefit from the experience of improvisation during the liturgy? What does it have to offer? What does it lack?
3. Does improvisation have an advantage or disadvantage over rehearsed, predetermined worship music—is there a risk factor in performing something in church that has never been heard before, as opposed to an old favorite that has the "stamp of approval"?

John Thorpe
The Protocol of Heaven: Liturgy and Ritual around God's Throne and Reflections of These in Christian Worship

This project is, in a sense, about what we ought NOT to do in worship, the proscriptive influence of the biblical pictures of the heavenly liturgy upon earthly Christian worship. Ritual studies tell us that the holiest things are often the most proscribed. In ancient Hebrew cult and culture, YHWH embodies both sovereignty and deity and in both aspects is understood as the subject of heavy protocol, particularly in scenes of God's throne. We will focus on protocols of access/approach, attitude, and activity.

The scenes of God's throne from Psalm 103, I Kings 22, Isaiah 6, Ezekiel 1-3 (also 10 and 43), and Daniel 7 express the understanding that God is properly the subject of restricted approach, reverent attitude, and specific activities. These, and these only, are appropriate; every other access, attitude, and activity represents a breach of heavenly protocol. To understand how these protocols may or may not influence Christian worship, we have to understand why Christian worship might be linked to the heavenly liturgy.

The New Testament Letter to the Hebrews provides this link. In it Christ is understood as interacting with the protocols of heaven successfully to obtain redemption for humanity. But more importantly, in Hebrews Christ has a continuing priesthood that makes it possible for every Christian to successfully negotiate the heavenly protocols, to "come boldly before the throne of grace." Christians are exhorted to understand their regular worship as coming before God's throne, where the protocols are still in place, but, because of Christ, do not keep people away.

Two examples of worship that take this link very seriously are Orthodox worship, which uses similar protocols around worship space, and Tabernacle worship, a structure of contemporary praise and worship in song that leads worshipers through five successive stages, culminating in an approach to the throne. Insofar as Christian worship is understood to be an approach to God's throne (not all worship need be understood this way), liturgical planners and leaders should be careful to observe the protocols of heaven somehow.

1. Biblical scholars today understand apocalyptic imagery differently from ancient writers: how might the need to observe heavenly protocols be understood differently without the traditional hermeneutic?
2. These protocols of access/approach, attitude, and activity all express power differentials.

How might this interact with a theology that rejects power differentials, particularly as a part of God's identity?

3.   How much is enough? If we are required to observe the protocols in worship, how fully must we observe them?

Katherine Trier
"The Great Speckled Bird"

The social climate of Appalachia is unique in that there is little distinction between the sacred and secular realms. Popular religiosity is defined as that part of faith construction that takes place outside of organized worship and is assimilated by the lay believer. "The Great Speckled Bird" is an example of a puzzle piece that I believe was used by Appalachian believers to enrich their faith lives.

"The Great Speckled Bird" has ambiguous origins but became popular when performed by Roy Acuff beginning in 1939 on the Grand Ole Opry. This marks an interesting point in history where the mass media served to reinforce the popular, local, religious culture of Appalachia, primarily defined as its fundamentalism. Fundamentalism is a phenomenon that transcends denominational lines and can be defined as (1) literal interpretation of Scripture; (2) separatist view of the world; (3) compromise = weakness. These characteristics were examined in the text of the hymn.

Also central to understanding Appalachian faith is the recognition that the everyday world is a world of power and that Appalachians exist in three realms of time simultaneously (the past, present, and future). Hence, participation in organized religion and unorganized informal events is empowering.

The separatist nature of fundamentalism arises out of the weight placed on literal interpretation of the Bible and the independence of churches and their formulations of doctrine. Many Appalachian pastors would identify one of the problems of the church as being blended with the world.

The last stanzas of the hymn focus on the imminence of the second coming of Christ and the importance of adhering to the church. It is a hymn about the preservation of the separateness of the church from the world, and about why it is important to "stand firm" to the church's teachings in the midst of outside pressure to compromise. "The Great Speckled Bird" still has a wide audience, is widely appreciated, and is illustrative of how the influence of the media can become a part of lay piety. I believe the reason for the hymn's popularity is that it speaks to Appalachian religious experience as a whole; it displays the major tenets of fundamentalism and affirms these choices. I believe "The Great Speckled Bird" tells us something about real life religion — that sometimes it is not about what people sing in church but what they hear around them that forms their religious belief.

1.   How can we assimilate popular religiosity into the worship services that we plan and carry out? What are the positives and negatives of doing this?

2.   How can dialogue between less and more conservative churches be facilitated?

3.   Are there other songs or aspects of culture that express your popular religiosity?

Jeffrey Wells
Worship and Justice: What is the Connection?

There has long been a biblically and theologically based assertion of a connection between Christian worship and Christian ethical formation for social justice. Liturgical scholars and practitioners in recent years have recognized that we cannot view such a connection by a linear model. Christian Scharen proposes an interactive model that sees a complex matrix of factors at work in forming communal identity and consequently communal ethical actions. Three important factors are congregational leadership (clergy and lay), theological orientation, and active membership participation. Congregations may embody the worship-justice connection both by expressing it in worship and by taking worship into their public justice work. Justice concerns can be expressed in worship through Scripture, prayers, music, sacramental signs and symbolic acts, and preaching. Justice is also expressed in more subtle ways through the makeup of a congregation, and how the membership is allowed or encouraged to participate in worship and congregational leadership and decision-making. Based on Scharen's studies of three Atlanta churches, and my own study of the Episcopal Church of St. Paul and St. James in New Haven, I concluded that in a congregation with a strong social-justice focus justice concerns are expressed in worship, although often in small and implicit ways. A strong justice focus in public worship does not seem to be required for a strong justice focus in the congregation's public work.

1. Is it legitimate to "use" worship as a vehicle to express social justice? That is, should there be a worship-justice connection?
2. What role can church musicians play in the formation of communal identity?
3. To what extent might more explicit and concrete expressions of justice in worship help to enhance the justice focus of a congregation whose commitment to social justice is weak?

Chris Wogaman
This is My Body, Broken: A Memorial Liturgy Following a Suicidal Death

I presented a Christian memorial/funeral liturgy that I have written for use after a suicidal death. I explored the area of how one might approach addressing emotions, particularly anger and guilt, explicitly in such a liturgy. As such, I intro-

duced a Confession and Forgiveness, as well as a Ritual of Tearing. I believe that more work needs to be done on liturgy around deaths by suicide, and other sudden, traumatic deaths, and that liturgy may have a pastoral-care component in being sensitive to such emotions. My own work in this area is just beginning, and I invite you to join me in this time of experimentation through this discussion.

1. What should the place of emotional expression be in a liturgy? Should it be explicitly written into the liturgy, or should emotions not be addressed in particular?
2. What effect did the Ritual of the Tearing have on you, or elicit in your imagination? Where else would you have placed it? Should such rituals be borrowed from other traditions?